A RABBI'S FAITH

SERMONS OF HOPE AND COURAGE

by

ABRAHAM A. KELLNER, M. A.

Rabbi, Congregation Sons of Abraham
Albany, New York

EARLE PRINTING CORPORATION
Albany, N. Y.

1945

Printing Statement:

Due to the very old age and scarcity of this book,
many of the pages may be hard to read due to the
blurring of the original text, possible missing pages,
missing text and other issues beyond our control.

Because this is such an important and rare work, we
believe it is best to reproduce this book regardless of
its original condition.

Thank you for your understanding.

To my dear Parents

With Love and Affection

ACKNOWLEDGEMENTS

It is with a sense of profound gratitude that I register my sincere thanks to those who made the publication of this humble volume possible.

Grateful appreciation is thus recorded:

To my honored colleagues who urged and encouraged me to undertake this publication.

To the men and women of my congregation and of the Jewish community in general who so loyally aided in the financing of this venture.

To the officers and members of the Sons of Abraham Book Fund, to all these and countless others, I acknowledge my indebtedness.

To my dear wife and helpmate in life, I cannot express my sentiments of gratitude in mere words for her ever ready helpfulness, constant inspiration, effective cooperation and patient criticism. Fortunately for me, King Solomon has provided for such an exigency, when he thus described a woman of valor and virtue:

"The heart of her husband trusteth in her and he hath no lack of gain."

Respectfully,

THE AUTHOR.

PREFACE

The speeches as printed in this collection were preached essentially as they appear in cold print, varying only in those essentials needed in transmuting the living word into blackface type.

But it is common knowledge that the effect of the spoken word depends for its success not only on the material preached but equally so upon the inspirational value which emanates from the enthusiasm and eloquence of the speaker.

These Sermons and Addresses follow a basic pattern as indicated by the sub-title. The tension and stress sired by the unhappy circumstances of wartime living made it imperative that if one was to preach at all, it would have to be done in a hopeful vein, in order to bring new strength to those wearied and worn by the tortured march of martyrdom endured by their fellowmen, the hapless victims of the unleashed forces of diabolical destruction.

Now more than ever is there cause to appreciate the Tadmudic dictum with reference to the origin of the name, "Ansher Kneseth Hagdoloh". Members of this saintly assembly earned their accolade because of their determination to enthrone Faith in an age shadowed by misery.[1] Deathlessness or immortality was their just reward for their indomitable will to proclaim their trust in God's all embracing Might at a time when the skyline of History was a flaming crimson painted by the flowing blood of martyrs. This will explain to the reader the general theme running through these sermons.

1. Talmud—Yoma 69B.

As the swift succession of events brought the war to
a most welcomed if unexpected close, I considered changing the introductory sermon, subsequent events however,
have more than amply proven that the burden of this
peroration is too tragically true.   Most of our loved ones
are still not at home and though we defeated Nazism in
the battlefield, we have still to win the battle against its
pernicious idealogy.

Unless otherwise indicated, these talks were delivered
at the Congregation Sons of Abraham, Albany, New York,
where it is my privilege to preach the Word of God.

The knowledge that these words may have lightened
the burden of even one lonely soul has amply compensated
my labours.

ABRAHAM A. KELLNER,

Albany, New York.

Cheshvan,   5706
October,   1945

FOREWORD

Not very often in the collection of books that roll off the printing presses do we find a volume dedicated to sermons. And the more welcome does it become because of kinship—it was dedicated to and for our synagogue and authored by our Rabbi, Abraham A. Kellner.

The Congregation is grateful to Rabbi Kellner, to Dr. Louis A. Lackey and to his committee for their sincere efforts in making this book and its distribution possible.

We also thank our many friends who by their generous subscriptions not only help to defray the cost of publication, but provided a fund for similar worthy congregational purposes.

NATHAN M. MEDWIN,

President.

TABLE OF CONTENTS

(xi)

xiv TABLE OF CONTENTS.

THE PEACE THAT TRUTH BUILDS

A Sermon for the First Day of Rosh Hashono

THOUGH the war-clouds in Europe have lifted, we are still enmeshed in a bloody war in the Pacific, and as much as we pray for its speeding conclusion, we are destined to say with the author of the Mishna: **Arboo roshe shonim hem.**[1] We are to have four war-time Rosh Hashono observances. For the fourth time, our solemn Festivals are tinged with the oppressive hues of tension and loneliness, painful longings, and unrequited hopes.

Rabbi Israel Salanter, of sainted memory, was fond of saying that the Good Lord created each of us with two eyes so that we could behold with one eye the noble qualities of our fellow humans, and with the other our own failings and shortcomings. In a like manner it is not amiss to state that on this sacred day we must register on the one hand our boundless gratitude for the privilege of Peace achieved in a part of the world at least, and on the other hand we must concern ourselves unremittingly with the faults and shortcomings, failures and limitations, that follow in the wake of the peace already achieved. Surely people will want to seek the road that will lead to permanent and universal peace for the sacrifice of blood and treasure that was expended in the prosecution of this horrible holocaust.

Those of us who listened to President Truman's reasoned and convincing plea to the San Francisco Conference must feel encouraged to believe that out of this cataclysmic chaos there must emerge the will and universal desire to begin building a new world. The choice

---

1. Talmud Rosh Hashono 2a.

(1)

is ours: The world called into being by Ten Heavenly
Pronouncements can be despoiled or maintained by the
peoples living in it.[2] Humanity's willingness to build
a new life or its inability to do so will be determined by
the outcome of our actions. Whether we reap the gains
or suffer the results of our deeds depends on each and
every one's efforts.

At the risk of being called a starry-eyed visionary, I
still hold to my firm belief that most of the people of
this earth anxiously await the coming of a better era
and consider the tensions and frictions, the storm and
stress, occasioned by the world-shaking events, as the
necessary pains and pangs that accompany the birth of
a new world life.

> Beat down yon beetling mountain
> And raise yon jutting cape;
> A world is on the anvil
> Now beat it into shape.

II

The achievement of world peace, though a most difficult task, is by no means impossible, and the procedure
for its attainment has been clearly outlined by the
prophet:

> "Thus hath said the Lord of Hosts, the fast of the
> fourth and the fast of the fifth, and the fast of the
> seventh, and the fast of the tenth, shall become to
> the House of Judah gladness and joy and merry
> festivals: only love ye the Truth and Peace." [3]

The Divine Seer of Israel here clearly projected the blue-

---

2. Aboth V, 1.
3. Zech. VIII, 19.

print that can turn the world's sorrows into jubilation, and he promulgated the essential principle which can guide us in building, upon the havoc wrought by the misdeeds of the past, a better integrated and more blissfully prosperous human society. The enthronement of Truth will effectively forge the instruments that can build the structure of peace, and it is for us to investigate the highway of perfection that will lead to the accomplishment of this desired end.

The instances in Holy Writ abound with timely reminders that all enduring accomplishments must be erected on the foundation of Truth, for falsehood hath no legs to stand upon. The traditional Biblical selection for today contains an inspiring example in that our forefather Abraham set forth in the search for Truth as an instrument of peace. We are told of the covenant that King Abimelech sought to establish with him. Before our illustrious grandsire proceeded with the consummation devoutly wished for, he reminded Abimelech of an evil act perpetrated by his minions:

> "And Abraham reproved Abimelech because of the well of water which Abimelech's servants had violently taken away." [4]

Our sainted Patriarch considered it advisable to speak the Truth even if it caused an embarrassing predicament rather than to suppress unpleasant mementoes and thereby sow the seeds for an inevitable future conflict.

Surely the leaders of mankind want to do nothing less today when the aching wounds of humanity cry out for healing. We will gain nothing by ignoring the fact that when this holocaust of fire was first unloosed upon the world, there was a tendency to view aggression in a de-

4. Genesis XXI, 25.

tached manner and with an attitude of indifference.
Now, when the world is about to constitute itself anew,
shall we cover up the crime of the nations who violently
deprived minorities within their borders and neighboring
peoples of the wells of living water that gave them sustenance and hope? Yea, we recall with sadness the fate
of Ethiopia whose doom was occasioned by the inflated
monster of Fascism. The world permitted this base
challenge to its decent impulses without even registering
a sincere gesture of protest. Spain was allowed to suffer
the convulsions of a ravaging Civil war, and the Democratic leaders of mankind stood by pronouncing pious platitudes whilst the dark denisons of dictatorships gave
murderous assistance to the bloody butcher of the Iberian
Peninsula. Pearl Harbor should not have come as such
a shocking surprise to those who watched with callous
disregard the dismemberment of China, an outrage which
began ten years before and constituted the first unchallenged aggression that rocked the foundations of the
laboriously erected structure of collective security.

There may be amongst us those who doubt the wisdom
of raking up the embers which smolder beneath the world
conflagration, but we must ever remember that we are
thinking in terms of building the world anew and only
then can we join the Act of Creation in effective association with the Creator, Blessed be He, if our pronouncements are true and our utterances are based on uncom-
promising Verities. The Sages of the Talmud anticipated such development when they told us in their beautifully impressive phraseology: **Kol dayon shedon din
emeth l'amitho shutof l'hakodash boruch hu.**[5] The victorious forces of Democracy could form this Divine Part-
nership if they but proceed in the way of Righteousness
and follow in the path of Justice.

---

5. Talmud, Shabbos 10.

III

The application of this principle is critically urgent in considering the solution of the painful problem of the homeless, the hounded, and the harrassed members of our Jewish people. Here again we must unequivocally state that when the barbaric atrocities were first visited upon our suffering co-religionists, the conscience of civilization was not too deeply mortified, and the nations of the earth seemed perfectly content to feed the unprotected Jew to the ravenous beast of Nazidom. Little did they consider that once having disposed of Israel, the monster would seek new victims to devour. Somehow people imagined that though a terrible fire consumed the homes of their neighbors, the conflagration would stop before it reached their possessions. The people that **Could** and **Should** have stopped this terrifying octopus before he spread his poisoned tentacles over half the globe, somehow believed that our world could continue half dark and half illuminated. With all the advancement of electrical science, we have as yet been unable to fashion the device that will darken part of a room while keeping the rest fully lighted. Had they but read Isaiah understandingly, they would have known: **Ki hineh hachoshech y'chase haaretz,**[6] that if darkness comes, it will cover the **whole** earth, **V'arofel l'umim,**[7] and when gross darkness rules supreme, it will effect **all** peoples.

If we are to pursue the Truth to the farthermost corners of the earth, we must recall on this day of Judgment that when the constituted leaders of humanity set out to right the wrongs of history after the First World War, they recreated Poland, established Chzechoslovakia,

---

6. Isaiah LX, 2.
7. Ibid.

ordained Yugoslavia into being, but to the long-suffering
children of Israel, only a promise was vouchsafed in the
form of the Palestinian Mandate—a promise which was
slowly whittled, limited, and circumscribed, culminating
in the infamy of last year's White Paper which blackened
the hope of a persecuted remnant and shut the door of
their Ancestral Land to them at a time when from every
country in Europe they were being driven forth with
merciless bestiality.   Jan Masryk, leader of the Chzecho-
slovakian delegation states:

> "It is my definite opinion that unless the Jewish
> problem is not only discussed by all concerned, but
> solved, the peace which we are endeavoring to in-
> itiate will not be complete. I have mentioned this
> to the leading statesmen assembled here, and I will
> continue to do so without let-up. Although I had
> nothing to do with the horror which befell your
> brave people, I feel personally co-responsible and I
> will never rest until the harm will be undone as
> much as possible."[8]

Our prayer is that this sentiment will be echoed by every
world-leader.

This self evident truth as well as the others effecting
the many nations of the World, must be unhesitatingly
bared, and the wounds thereof healed before we can
rebuild the world. If the leaders of the world will be
possessed of the moral courage and endowed with intellectual forthrightness to face the truth unflinchingly,
they will thereby place themselves in the vanguard of
those brave and chosen souls who in the words of the
Mishna are actually helping to establish and sustain the
world which was called into being by the Ten Sacred
Utterances of our Creator.

---

8. **The Day** July 1st, 1945, Page 6.

In every critical period when upon the ruins of a collapsing civilization a new one was erected, the application of our principle was clearly needed. The disaster which threatened to engulf our ancestors during the time of Mordecai and Esther was barely averted when the good queen sent information to the people of her faith throughout the Empire and impressed them with the necessity of enthroning Truth when they sought to establish Peace. Coupling these two ideals, she spoke to her people of: **Divrei shalom v'emeth**[9]—"The words of Truth and Peace."

This thought is even more clearly emphasized in the words of Rabbi Simon ben Gamliel who teaches us that:

"By three things is the world preserved: by Truth, by Judgment, and by Peace."[10]

This lesson if appropriately applied will bring nearer the realization of our enchanted dream. The Sage speaks of Emeth first, and we have developed its importance in reestablishing moral relations between the inhabitants of the world. Next must come the stern application of **Din**, Justice. In the hour of triumph, the victors must not forget that Justice means both recompense wherever possible for the hapless victims of Hitlerism, as well as justly meted-out punishment to the perpetrators of the unspeakable atrocities witnessed in our day. We will not serve the cause of humanity, nor the purposes of Peace, if we fail to deal with just severity, with those who drenched the world in blood and in tears. These two ideals will then bring about the final consummation of the third, which is the hope of every heart, and which will reach out into all the shadowy areas of sorrow where the cruel inhumanity of man has placed his less fortunate

9. Esther, IX, 30.
10. Aboth I, 18.

fellows. Only by making such a peace will we have woven forever into the great vibrating web of the world our dreams of a social order where sincerity shall supplant perfidy, where the corroding rust of want and need shall not cover the land, where the persecution of the weaker, the proscription against minorities, the oppression by the strong, approbrium by the mighty, shall be banished into oblivion, because men will judge with Truth, and the Judgment of Peace will be in their gates.[11]

> Whence come this iron music
> Whose sound is heard afar?
> The hammers of the world's smiths
> Are beating out a star.

---

11. Zech. VIII, 16.

THE TOMORROWS THAT SING

Preached on the Second Day of Rosh Hashono, 5705

M Y FRIENDS, the festive sermon is once more based on the ever new story of Abraham's pilgrimage to Mount Moriah. I bespeak your kind interest in one minor episode of this stirring epic, which, if properly evaluated will help us enormously to face with equanimity the trials and vicissitudes with which we are daily confronted.

Thus we read that when our ancestor advanced resolutely to keep his appointed date with destiny, he lifted up his eyes **Vayar eth hamokom merochok**—"And he saw the place from the distance."[1] In this simple narrative is concealed more than words can tell, and more than the ordinary human eye can see. In that longing gaze of Abraham to a place far off lay concealed the seeds of a reassuring hope which could well serve our weary and war-worn generation. Abraham taught us by his own example to look beyond the misty haze of the present and to seek salvation in the unrevealed mysteries of the future. He blazed a trail which has enabled the stouthearted ever since to rise above the burden of the immediate and find solace in the enchantment of things in distant view. Though his circumstances were marked by abject terror and his situation was fraught with complete resignation, yet, by the sheer strength of his soul and by the unyielding hope of his heart, he envisioned redemption by fixing his gaze steadily forward. "And he saw the place from Far Off."

The Rabbis of the Midrash were the first to grasp the

---

1. Genesis 22, 4.

(9)

profound significance of Abraham's experience, and they
fortify this observation with the following remarkable
allegory. They tell us that Abraham, when he looked
ahead, asked his son Isaac to record his impression of
the Distant place and Isaac replied,

> "I see a pleasant hill ahead, with an overhanging
> cloud from above." [2]

Abraham then turned to the servants who accompanied
them and asked them the same question, but they reported
that all they saw was desert and desolation. Aye, my
friends, the eye of man's spirit could direct him Godward
and make him see beyond the bleak realities of the
present—the promise of great adventure. Man can, if
inspired, fix his vision upon **distant** horizons and behold
a majestic mountain where heaven and earth meet in
fond embrace through overhanging clouds hovering above.
If one is blinded to the higher verities of man's destiny,
then these heartening tendencies of his current misfor-
tunes will appear as unrelieved desolation and bleakness;
if, however, he is endowed with a constant and invariable
hope to believe in the shining sun even when the skies
are laden with terror, then the inner depths of his soul
will instinctively react against the horror of his environment and will lead him to the path which in the words
of the prophet will enable him to span the chasm: **M'emek
ochar l'petach tikvoh**—"From the valley of despair to
the dale of Hope." [3]

The cultivation of such a hopeful attitude empowers
one to perceive the sustaining Hand of Providence even
when he walks in the valley of the Shadow of Death.
Such a heightened awareness of the Omnipresence of a
Loving God enables the strong in heart to catch a glimpse

---

2. Ibid., Tanchuma.
3. Hosea, 2, 17.

of eternity by remaining steadfast with the highest ideals of humanity, by displaying consistently the deepest sentiment of devotion to all moral considerations, by indulging in the finest expressions of beauty about God's Will and the purposes of creation, and by reacting with the noblest manifestations of holiness to every experience in life.

The disciples of God thus equipped become the heroes of the spirit who in their times have written large the saga of their days. These are people who do not despair when the train of logic stops but direct their eyes heavenward and clear the impediments that clog the way to Godliness. Their armor is deeply imbedded in the hope of their hearts and in the implicit trust reposing in their souls. There are few words, my friends, in any language that can equal the calm and strength that exudes from the simple word **Hope**. The sound of its music surpasses the delicate notes of an Aeolian harp whose softly enchanting strains quiver in the calm of a summer twilight, thus becoming one with the enticing harmony of nature and with the stirring symphony of the universe. Where hope reigns supreme the sun shines brighter, the moonbeams reflect a softer glow, the stars dazzle more radiantly, the birds sing sweeter songs, and the flowers of life shed more fragrant blossoms. This attitude is like a divine instrument which plays on a thousand strings whose sounds mend the pain of a broken heart and ease one's path toward **Life** triumphant.

II

Our sacred literature is filled with the drama of heroes, who, though enmeshed in pain and sorrow or entangled in a web of circumstance, were still able to summon the fortitude latent in their souls to rise above the frighten-

ing futility of their immediate environment.   Their
choice was thus described by a poet

> "Two people looked out from prison bars
> One looked down and saw the mud
> The other looked up and saw the stars."

Those whose courage impels them to look up and see a
ray of hope radiating from the brilliant luminaries of the
skies, merely emulate the example of our forefather who
also looked up and saw a splendid hill.

Miriam, of a later generation, stood hopefully by, while
her little brother was placed in the bulrushes.   And
whilst the circumstances surrounding that act would
have occasioned bitter despair if faced by less hardy
souls, the prophetess, like Abraham before her, invoked
a Distant view and faced the future unflinchingly.   Her
hope too was predicated upon expectations that resided
in the hazy mist of things to be.   As Scripture so point-
ingly remarks: **Vatesatzav achoso merochok**—"And his
sister stood from afar." [4]   The same word, the same
hope, the same courage thus sustained Miriam in her hour
of great trial.

III

No less exalting was the solace emanating from the
fiery soul of Jeremiah.   He also lived in historic times,
and he too needed every ounce of his flaming spirit to
look beyond the vale of tears and mountain of sorrows
that engulfed him.   As he listened to the sledgehammer
blows of Israel's adversary resounding on the city walls,
and as the impending doom of his people became im-
minent, he reassuringly proclaimed his unconquerable

---

4. Exodus 2, 4.

hope: **Merochok hashem nireh li**—"The Lord appears unto me from a **Distance**." [5] And as the prophet perceived in Him the promise of ultimate blessings, he knew that the loving care of God would forever be extended to him. **V'ahavath olam ah autich**—"For I have loved Thee with perrennial love."[6] Blessed are the mortals unto whom the capacity for such vision is vouchsafed and who thus are enabled to transmute the hideous realities of the present into promising ideals of the future. This prophetic power found expression in diverse forms and manifested itself in numerous fashions. Unto Abraham and Isaac it appeared in the form of a magnificent mountain. Jacob envisioned it as a ladder that reached the very skies. Moses perceived it in the Burning Bush. Solomon heard the word of God in a nocturnal vision. Elijah felt it in a soft still Voice. Isaiah caught a glimpse of eternity in a Flaming Chariot, and Jeremiah reaffirmed his faith by transacting a seemingly commonplace property transaction, whose exalted purpose was to reassure the dismayed in heart that they will still buy homes, plow fields, and plant vineyards in the land of their fathers.[7]

We can find redemptive qualities in the tragic chapter of humanity's travail as it is fashioned today, if we look beyond the shadows that envelope us and catch a glimpse of Truth Eternal that shines above the cavalcade of passing events like the gleam of a tranquil star that takes refuge from the darkness beyond the reach of drifting clouds.

IV

These, my friends, are perhaps but fugitive thoughts which may make little or no impression upon the minds

5. Jeremiah 31, 2.
6. Ibid.
7. Ibid., 32, 15.

and hearts of my listeners. Surely they will tell me that beautiful words and eloquent orations will not cure the world of its weighty and chronic ills, but the truth, if declared, and its message if emphasized and its meaning repeatedly proclaimed, may help some to understand that life's greatest need, man's most compelling necessity, civilization's most urgent obligation; is to interpret properly the impact of our times and to discern in the rhythm of the cosmic forces unloosed about us an inherent promise of faith in the ultimate goodness of humanity that will transform our weeping yesterdays into singing tomorrows.

The story is told about one of the leaders of the French Underground who was captured by the dreaded Gestapo. Knowing full well the fate that faced him, he managed to send a farewell note to his sister's son who was his trusted lieutenant in their dangerous exploits. In this moving epistle he urged his nephew to continue the work undauntedly for the liberation of their people. "I beg you," he said, "to dedicate yourself, your life and your hopes to the tomorrows that will sing, to the future that will bring liberation."

The farewell message of this martyr to a great cause rings in our ears as we too are called upon to translate the heartbreak of the present into a willingness to work for the betterment of mankind, which will herald the rise of a better dawn.

I ask you, sisters and brethren, to believe with me in the tomorrows that will sing, to believe that out of the chaos and confusion caused by the cruel abominations of a demolished domain, that out of the sorrow and suffering that walk in the wake of global war, that out of the debris of desolation that is the tragic concomitant of the powers of destruction, that out of all these tragic manifestations and harrowing experiences will emerge the forces of peace and unity that will burst terrestrial bounds, mending the broken fragments of man with the age old and never tarnished assurance: **Shalom shalom larochok v'la korav omar hashem u'rfoosiv.**[8]

---

8. Isiah 57, 19.

THE TRUTH THAT GIVETH LIFE

Preached on the First Day of Rosh Hashono, 5704
Sons of Abraham Congregation, Albany, N. Y.

THE sum and substance of the prayers recited on this hallowed day is expressed in the repeated refrain of the ritual

"Remember us for Life, O King Who delightest in Life;[1] Inscribe us in the Book of Life, Thou King of Life."

All of us would no doubt grasp the opportunity if offered to be certain of the bounty of life in return for some price exacted, some compensation demanded, or some recompense called for. Our Sages in the Talmud speak of just such an opportunity when they relate the remarkable incident of the vendor who paraded in the streets of ancient Tiberias and plaintively asked

"Who is desirous of obtaining an elixir of Life?"[2]

Then he remarked:

"Keep thy tongue from evil and thy lips from speaking falsehood."[3]

Not a very exacting price for the blessings of Life, one would be led to remark, but it is a prerequisite that certainly ought to be insisted upon before we storm the Heavens with our heartrending pleas for life and its joys.

It behooves us to ask the pertinent question, "Do we observe the command of the psalmist? Do we tell the

---

1. High Holy Day Machzor.
2. Talmud; Abodah Zarrah, 79b.
3. Psalms XXXIV, 14.

truth in our daily transactions, in our every-day inter-
course with our fellowmen? Nay, more than that, in
our religious life, in our attendance, in our Holiday
prayers and sacred exercises do we guard our tongues
from evil?" Surely our affirmations and acknowledg-
ments are in a sense betraying falsehoods if they are not
in consonance with our daily needs. A Jew who beats
his breast in registering the confession of his sins during
the Holy Day Season, and then continues cheerfully in
the mode of life to which he has been accustomed during
the rest of the year, is most certainly not speaking the
Truth to his God!

As we gaze into the heavens that hide the secret mysteries of the future, we wonder what the New Year will
be like and what it will bring to us and to those so dearly
beloved by us. The Rabbi, however, furtively inquires,
is our New Year going to be but a replica of yesteryear
or is our affirmation of our faith to be kept in earnest and
will the utterances of our lips bespeak the truth and will
the new season actually see a new evaluation of our
spiritual lives? Particularly at this time, as the terrible
uncertainties of war are shaking our established mores
to their very foundations, these perplexing questions are
pregnant with added meaning. Are we so callously cynical that even now Rosh Hashono will mean crowded synagogues for two days and empty pews for three hundred
and sixty-three, or will the world-disturbing happenings
which we are experiencing arouse a dormant people from
their lethargic stupor and cause them to really speak
the truth in their Holy Day prayers and help find them
a new interest in their ageless experience of religious
devotion and spirituality? Will they find satisfying
raith in a new devotion to spiritual ideas, new loyalties
to an ancient faith, and a new love for the Eternal? Or
will the New Year be new to us in a chronological sense
only, and not by a spiritual cleansing and a new set of

values? If so we are not really interested in the enchanting elixir of life as we do not understand or speak the spiritual truths necessary for its possession. If we really change our accepted modes of life and train ourselves to return to the true and tested moorings of our faith, then we will indeed partake of the truth which is the surest guarantee of life.

In the sacred ritual of the day, we find a beautiful illustration of a method suggested whereby we can make the New Year everlastingly new. The author of the plaintive, haunting prayer envisioned the awesome effects of this Holy Day by conjuring up a Heavenly scene in which even the Angels tremble as they behold the workings of Divine Justice: **Umalochim yechofezun.** The high spot of this Heavenly panorama is reached when in the words of the composer:

> "A blast of the mighty horn will be sounded and a small still voice will be heard."[4]

Strange consequence indeed! The blow issues forth from a mighty instrument and the voice registering it is soft, small, still, and subdued. These words were no doubt borrowed from Elijah's experience in the desert. He, too, just as many a downcast spirit of today **Vayvakesh eth nafsho lomuth**—"Sought death as an antidote for his spiritual anguish."[5] A moving vision, a soul-stirring spectacle restored his sorely tried soul as, in rapid succession: A mighty wind blew that reached the terrifying proportions of a hurricane, but when he eagerly leaned forward to perceive the Word of God in the stormy wind, the Voice of God was not to be heard in the wind; and earthquake of terrifying immensity followed, shattering the very foundations of earth, but when the Pro-

4. High Holy Day Machzor.
5. Kings I, Chapter 19, verse 4.

phet anxiously peered into the abyss in order to discern
the Word of God in this unusual phenomenon, the Word
of God was not revealed in the quake; and then occurred
an all-consuming fire that seemingly would consume all
before it, but when Elijah advanced toward it to
divine in the irridescent glow of this world conflagration
a Heavenly Message, no, not even the mighty fire was the
vehicle which conveyed the Word of God. A still, small
Voice was heard after these manifestations of power and
immensity—this still small Voice was the implement of
God's revelation, and it was the still, small Voice that
murmured in soothing accents to the weary soul of the
sorely tried prophet.

My people, the noisy blasts of the enemies of mankind,
the fiery holocaust which consumes so many of our people,
the disturbances and dislocations that mark our tragic
period, are not the manifestations of the Godly Voice;
the soft still Voice of hope that wells up within every one
of us and the hushed and stilled voices of our heroes who
become martyrs in lands of sorrow and death, God hears
them though the world does not and will not. God
hearkens and will give our answer soon.

In the same manner in our Jewish life, we often fall
victim to the illusion that the noise and tumult engendered by the Rosh Hashono Services are the evident
manifestations of the Divine Presence. In truth the
mighty blast, soon to be issued from the Shofar, the
appealing prayer of the Cantor, yea even the oratorical
thunderings of the preacher are but and should be considered only the prelude—the wind, the fire, and the
earthquake which prepare the way for the soft still Voice
of our conscience. Surely Rosh Hashono would degenerate into "much ado about nothing" were it not to produce
some lasting effect, some beneficial result, something of
an enduring value.

3

We must take care that the majestic accents of our Divinely appointed Day should be heard, understood, and clearly discerned, or else its meaning will be lost in the maze of events surrounding our observances. Just as a man does not build a new house without first employing an architect, so it is that the Rosh Hashono ceremonial is but the blue print, the plan and design, for the New Year whose foundations we place today in our souls. The finest blueprint will become useless unless it is translated into reality; the noblest resolve today is of no import; the most moving service is of no avail; the most inspiring Shofar ceremony of no moment, unless it is considered as the Chochmoh—the intelligent plan to build one's spiritual life all the year around. Our Sages imparted a warning and did not simply indulge in symbolic description when they proclaimed that **Tekiath shofar chochmoh veinoh m'lochoh.**

"The Blowing of the Shofar is an art, not a task."[6]

The blowing of the Shofar is the attractive blueprint which will become useless unless it is understood in relation to the rest of the Plan. If it is recognized as a summons to action, a call to duty, and, to be effective, followed up by the **M'lochoh**—which in the Still, small Voice will make us aware of our responsibilities toward our Faith and our Creator the year around, **that** will put the blueprint into action and translate the Plan into a reality.

The Voice of the Shofar today will be heard all over the world, in myriads of places. The underground caves and the hidden cellars will resound to the call of the Shofar in terror-stricken Europe. The frozen wastes of the Aleutians and the burning sands of the Sahara Desert will hear the ancient notes. The rolling waves of the high seas will echo the summons issuing from the Ram's Horn

---

6. Talmud Rosh Hashono.

and even in the depths of the seas, wherever our Boys will be, the stirring sounds of the call of Freedom will once again be a reminder that our people were once enslaved and then freed by the Holy One, Blessed be His Name, and this miracle will happen again.   On this day, in response to the Shofar, Jewish men everywhere will rally to Freedom's call and await the day of redemption, when in the words of the Prophet and in answer to the vibrations of the Shofar:

> "Those who were lost in the land of Assyria and those who were banished to the shores of Egypt will return with joy and bow before the Lord in the Holy City of Jerusalem."
>
> Amen.

SO PROUDLY WE GIVE

Preached on the Second Day of Rosh Hashono, 5704

MANY of us conceive of Rosh Hashono as being set aside for us specifically for the purpose of asking for the gift of life and its blessings. This conception would mark man as a beggar at the gates of Heaven whose only concern is for the thing he may obtain and plead for at the Hands of an All Merciful Creator.

Judaism in its pristine understanding places a far greater emphasis on giving than on receiving. More than for our carefully enunciated pleas, requests, and supplications, the spirit of these high holy days calls for a Cheshbon Hanefesh, for thorough self-searching and soul analysis. One must square his spiritual accounts on this day and see how much he has contributed to life. Was his contribution in the same measure as that which he is prepared to take? Did he, who is anxious to receive, sufficiently give? Did he emphatically contribute to the cause of human happiness in order that his participation may help in the enthronement of God in human affairs?

The Bible indeed records the story of one person whose all-consuming ambition and all-pervading desire was to be a recipient, to take, to enjoy, and to share in, in fuller measure than he was entitled to, the pleasure and prominence which bring fleeting joy to mortal man. The very words with which Holy Writ introduces the tale of this adventurer begin with "Vayikach Korach" "and Korah Took", a severe indictment and a condemning summation with which the attitude and desire of this individual were expressed. The rabbis in the Tanchumah rightfully comment:

[22]

"He took himself by his avarice out of the community."[1]

Overcome by his blind desire, he effectually moved his presence from the camp of Israel and took himself out from the Congregation of God.

Giving is more in harmony with Jewish religious ideals than taking, as is so picturesquely reflected in the Scriptural lesson assigned for the day. In it we read anew the deathless story of our forefather Abraham and his readiness to sacrifice upon the altar of the highest love imaginable the one dearest to his heart. Today, when our blood and treasure is so willingly offered for the maintenance of our ideals and the welfare of mankind, God's Call to our ancestor sounds especially timely: **"Kach no et bincho"**—"Take thy son thy beloved one".[2]

To those unto whom this episode appeared fantastically exaggerated and needlessly cruel, the experience of our own times renders it meaningful. Now when to millions of American homes has come the call, "Send thy Son and thy Daughter", that they too may scale the majestic hills of devotion, the heights of inspired idealism, and the lofty peaks of patriotic duty, we can readily comprehend that the adventure of Abraham was but the pattern planned in the High Heavens to serve as an example for later generations.

It was to serve as an irrevocable impression upon the hearts of men to remind them in times of crises, in moments of disaster not unlike ours that we should be prepared, as was Abraham, to cheerfully send forth the dearest among us to do battle for God, Country and humanity.

---

1. Numbers 16, 1.
2. Genesis 22, 2.

Yes, we have given; we give, and that regardless of cruel injustice, baseless slander, wicked criticism, and ferocious onslaughts. We give our best means, our highest endeavors, our noblest efforts, our deepest sentiments, our most precious possessions, on the altar of patriotism. Now, as on no other occasion, when Israel's great ideal of sacrificial giving is read anew at our Divine Services in every Synagogue throughout the land, we defiantly proclaim that **so proudly we give** our share and more than our share for our country's defense, and we hurl the challenge to the cowardly forces of evil that seek to undermine the unity of the home front by driving a wedge between the diverse stratas of American Life.

This basic characteristic of the Jewish ideal of service is, like the divine attributes of the Almighty Lord,[3] stated in Pentateuch, restated in Prophets, and three-fold emphasized in Writings. It is exemplified in countless Biblical incidents and I will select one from each of the divisions of Holy Writ to indicate that **selfless devotion** is manifest in the lives of all of our Biblical heroes and that its supremacy in human offerings reflects from every line of our Sacred Literature.

The mission of Israel has been from the days of Abraham to give bread to a hungry world. Our forefather indeed lavishly proffered victuals to every person who chanced to go by the door of his tent; his descendants carried on his teachings by offering to famished humanity Divine Bread, or, the Word of the Law. In the fourth chapter of the second Book of Kings we read that thrilling story of Elisha the Prophet and his acceptance of twenty loaves of bread from an admirer. Does he consider for a moment keeping the bread for himself? No, he forthwith dispensest the food: **"Vayomer ten lo hem vayechalu."**

---

3. Talmud Megillah 31.

And he said "Give it unto the people and let them eat, for thus saeth the Lord."[4]

In this sublimely stirring statement is delineated Israel's purpose in the world—not a place in the sun as other nations have construed their destiny, not an anxious ambition to rule the world by might as despotic tyrannies have attempted from time immemorial, not a fierce passion to subjugate nations and take their possessions, no, Israel is happy in the fact that it is giving something to the world. A timeless truth to tell, an invaluable service to render, a prophetic mission to deliver, a deathless message to preach, an abiding principle to enunciate, these and countless others like these have constituted the burden that Israel carries on the high road toward human ennoblement. Other religious have sprung from its womb and were nurtured on its strength, yet Israel rests assured and is content to feed disciple nations just as Elisha nourished his pupils. **L'hatalmidins shehoyo zion.**[5] Spreading before a famished world a table full of spiritual victuals does not deprive Israel of its own food for survival, for indeed, **"V'hosir."** The vast limitlessness of our Divine Law leaves enough also for our own soulful consumption.

This desire of Israel to share with the rest of mankind its cultural treasures has been beautifully illustrated by the Midrashic comment upon a fugitive description in King Solomon's immortal Song of Songs. In comparing Israel's soul to different natural phenomena, the royal poet exclaims: **"K'tapuach b'atzei hayaar."**

"As an apple tree amongst the trees of the Forest."[6]

The Rabbis of the Midrash whose minds were quickened

---

4. Kings 2, IV, 42.
5. Ibid., Rashi.
6. Songs of Songs 2, 3.

by every suggestive phrase of Holy Writ tenderly added:
"Mah tapuach piru okodem."

> "Just as an apple tree produces fruitful blossoms be-
> fore the full fruition of the leaves, so did Israel
> accept the burden of the Torah, before its contents
> were explained and enunciated."[7]

To this inspiring homily one may add that Israel's burdensome task of bringing to the world the fruits of its
"Eitz Chaim" began before the leaves of his tree had
fairly started to grow. A people that was not even
settled on its own land, a nation whose national characteristics were not defined in the customary terminology of
landed possessions but in the "Kingdom of Priesthood and
Holiness", a folk that had had no time as yet to settle
securely upon its ancestral soil, was already dispensing
Divine Bread and distributing Heavenly Manna to all who
were desirous of it; a nomadic people that suffered im-
measurable degrees of injustice was only too ready to
teach an unwilling world its first lesson in righteousness
and justice.

That the world is not anxious to register gratitude,
worse yet, that it is heaping ignominy and persecution
upon the anguished head of Israel, is but the world's treat-
ment of Prophets. Israel, the classic prophet of the nations, will not be dismayed if her recompense is not forthcoming in the ordinary terms of reward and appreciation.
Our deepest satisfaction must come from the realization
that we always dreamed of kindling the lights of humanity rather than of darkening its cloudy horizons. As
torch-bearers of enlightenment, we were of course, always
confronted with and opposed by the arrayed forces of evil
unto which the beacon lights of civilization are an impedi-
ment and an obstacle. Only too well do we remember the
story that is told of the small-town European Jew in the

---

7. Ibid., Yalkut Shemoni.

19th Century who lived at the edge of his village where the roads from the different communities converged. During his old age, when he was no longer able to work, he cast about for some way in which he could be of some use or benefit to his fellowmen. He was too poor to give charity, and totally unlearned for giving instruction. So he decided to equip himself with lamps and lanterns to be of service to passersby and to carriages or wagons that rode by his humble home. The roads were unpaved, and travelling was indeed very dangerous, especially after dark. One night, after he had already retired, our friend heard a terrific noise in the distance. Fearing that a mishap had occurred to a passing carriage, he rushed to the scene and discovered several men busily engaged in an attempt to break down the iron bars of a store. Anxious to be of service, our hero lifted his lantern to throw light upon their faces. At once the men fell upon him and beat him severely. When he protested his good will and his desire to be of service, they sarcastically informed him: "We are robbers, we must do our work in the dark; if you put your light here, we will be prevented from carrying out our purpose. Light is our enemy, Darkness is our Friend." No wonder Israel has always been marked for darkness by the purveyors of evil and darkness.

Aye, my friends, the Jew will continue undaunted to Give to Mankind the Light of the Torah, the Light of Prophetic teachings, the Light that flames forth from the souls of martyred heroes. We were never guilty of lowering the flame of man's hopes, patiently awaiting the coming of the day when the world will be imbibe the refreshing waters of God's Law and, in the words of Isaiah, will thus bring bright cheer into the tired hearts of all God's children when "Nations shall walk in Thy Light and Kings in the brightness of Thy rising."[8]

---

8. Isaiah 60, 3.

HOME THOUGHTS FROM THE SYNAGOGUE

Preached on Yom Kippur Eve., 5705

THE Hallowed Spirit of Yom Kippur Eve which creates the blessed homelike atmosphere in the Synagogue is particularly conducive to the enunciation of some truthful homilies and the preaching of a simple message that can find its way into the hearts of the listeners. I find myself speaking to my brothers and sisters tonight, not as the stern magistrate of admonition, but rather as an older member of your household who addresses a family reunion and who points to the urgent tasks which need immediate attention.

The peculiar circumstances incident to our daily lives have occasioned far-reaching changes in the daily expression of Jewish life, many of which, while in themselves edifying, may become the focal points of inherent danger. To quote but one example, every traditional Synagogue in our land erects a Sukkah on the Feast of Tabernacles. Some indeed take great care to make the Festive Booth a thing of beauty and a source of inspiration. A great deal of loving care is thus lavished upon this seasonal event and very often our young ones are initiated into the religious practices of our faith with their early participation in the decoration of the Booth. This otherwise splendid custom has, however, made the Home Sukkah almost nonexistent. Thus a complete generation of American Jews will grow up hardly knowing the necessity of observing the Mitzvah by having a family Tabernacle. In a similar manner we discharge our obligations with the use of Congregational Esrog. Lately, many Synagogues ape the Reform Temple by arranging for a public Seder.

[28]

More and more of the practices of the home are being transferred into the public houses of worship.

No one would knowingly challenge the centrality of the Synagogue in Jewish Life, our refuge and our fortress from ages past.   Surely our place of worship has become invested with sanctity and wholesomeness, but it falls short of its hallowed goal if it fails to imbue our daily lives with the beauty and dignity of inspired existence. The House of God has ever been the Shrine of self examination and inner solitude where the soul of the Jewish people repaired for solace and encouragement when the impact of daily living caused their spiritual beings to become bruised and sore due to the constant abrasion of mounting tension.   Here in this quiet, the dust of the worldliness about the individual Jew could be shaken from his overburdened and weary soul.   Our Place of Prayer does indeed compare with the high places of the earth and one can readily envision our House of Worship as a lofty mountain, a majestic, towering eminence, about which the rarified atmosphere exudes holiness.

"And upon the high mountain shall be their fold"[1] sayeth the prophet.

Where one can feel the nearness of God and the Majestic Sweep of His Creation, and where Nature Itself worships the Maker of the Universe, Nature enshrouded in the glistening robes of the High Priests' white vestments. Still, this truly magnificent aspect of Jewish religious adventure fails to express the "summum bonum" of our spiritual aspirations.

In the symbolic word play of our Sages' Jewish life, portrayed in the lofty prayer of a towering mountain range is by itself inadequate:

---

1. Ezekial XXXIV, 14.

"It will not be expressed solely by the Picturesque-
ness of Abraham's experience on the hillside."[2]

Pray we do, and pray we must, but prayer service alone
is not the answer to the aching problems of American
Israel. If the Synagogue fails to inspire us to a deeper
consciousness of and a wider participation in Jewish life,
then it will be only like an imposing mountain whose
grandeur is awesome but whose very appearance bespeaks
an immobile and lifeless existence.

In a thoroughly integrated Jewish Life, inspired by a
higher yearning and a deeper vision, our fondest prayers
are but the broad base upon which the structure of our
faith is established. When upon this solid foundation of
faith and worship is erected a vibrant and penetrating
religious life, then the mountain is not a barren rock but
a lush forest, carpeted by the strong unifying and protecting faith of our beliefs. These enveloping traditions
are constantly illuminated by the steady glow of hope and
inspiration derived from our participation in Synagogue
life, which brightens the heavy shadows cast upon the
forest of Jewish living by a misunderstanding and hostile
world.

"Break forth into singing, O ye mountain, forest, and
every tree therein."[3]

II

Another manifestation of our religious activities is the
growing importance attached to our schools of religious
learning, the Talmud Torahs and Yeshivas. Here too the
American Synagogue made a splendid though incomplete
beginning. Faulty and halting, inadequate and short-

2. Talmud Pesachim 88a.
3. Isaiah 44, 23.

sighted as most of our Synagogue Hebrew Schools have been, they nevertheless blazed the trail and established the historical continuity which from the earliest times honored the Jewish House of Prayers also as a:

"A House of Learning and Study".[4]

as a place where the treasured legacy of our Sainted martyrs is planted into the hearts of our young ones. Jewish education is a much abused field of religious endeavor, a field where care should be taken that the seeds so painstakingly planted in the bosom of mother earth should sprout forth in splendid shoots and rich growth. The Prophet indeed, in speaking of a field, joins it together with the seeds that ought to grow therein.

History records that in time of famine the tillers of the soil planted in the rich humus of the earth the last precious measure of carefully guarded wheat, although the members of their families were on the brink of starvation. Similarly must we expend the last ounce of our strength, the last measure of our devotion, on the carefully nurtured fruits of our communities and congregations. We should devote ourselves to the task of planting in the field of our educational endeavors the seeds that will bear fruit in the form of cultured and historically trained youth steeped in the ideals of our ancient heritage.   Thus will the generations of our people continue in the words of Ezekial's prophecy:

"Myriads like the vegetation of the field have I made thee."[6]

---

4. Talmud Berochoth 64a.
5. Jeremiah 35, 9.
6. Ezekial 16, 7.

III

The living symbol portrayed by the fields looms large
in our concepts but even these fail to express in full the
symphony of Jewish life as it should be depicted and carried on from generation to generation. The work of our
fields, the schools, is of incalculable significance, but, left
to itself, it too falls short of our goal: **V'lo k'yitzchok
shekosuv bo sodeh.** The finest of schools, the most
thoroughgoing of institutions would be of no avail if the
precepts taught and the lessons inculcated are not put
into practice in our homes. The Scripture enjoins every
Jew to instruct his children in the Laws of God. While
it is not practicable for every individual parent to turn
pedagogue, it is incumbent upon him to arrange for instruction at an available place of instruction. Thus the
Bible speaks in the plural sense when this Commandment
is affirmed:

> "And ye shall teach them diligently unto thy chil-
> dren."[7]

Yet immediately thereafter, Holy Writ continues:

> "To speak to them when thou sittest in thy house
> and when thou walkest by the way."[8]

The transition to the singular is made without apparent
reason. Our commentators excellently justify it by re-
minding us that whilst for instruction we may send our
young ones to School, for the practice of their learning
we must provide them the opportunity in our homes.
Every Jew who walks the high road of life and treads the
path that leads to glory and every Jewess that reigns over
her household and sets the tone for practices therein must

---

7. Deuteronomy 6, 7.
8. Ibid.

constantly and continually utilize every opportunity to translate into deeds the theoretical knowledge absorbed in school. The zenith of Jewishness will be attained only if it radiates from the Synagogue where we pray with all our hearts, through the school where Jewish consciousness is strengthened and the content of Jewish knowledge is deepened, and climaxed in the home where Judaism should be lived. **Elo k' yaakov sher kosuv bo bayis.**[9]

Only if the symbol of the home as reflected in the life of Jacob were re-established in its pristine beauty and strength can the full symphony of Jewish life be played in our lives.

Then will this, our Synagogue, like Jacob's ladder of dreams, become indeed a House of God through which we send our fondest prayers to the very Gates of Heaven to our Merciful Father Who dwelleth high above the praise of Israel now and forever.

---

9. Talmud Pesachim 88a.

THREE YEARS OF FAMINE

Yiskor Sermon Preached at Congregation Beth El Jacob,
Albany, New York, Yom Kippur Morning, 5705

WE ARE participating this morning in our third wartime Yom Kippur Yiskor Service. This devotional exercise is thus necessarily shadowed with more than its usual share of melancholy moods and sorrowful remembrances. The painful record of wartime losses, augmented so heavily by the destruction wrought upon European Jewry, causes us to mourn this morning more than our own personal sorrows and anguish would warrant.

This grievous milestone recalls a remarkable incident which is related in the Book of Samuel and which has a poignant significance for this day: **Vayhi roov b'ymei dovid sholosh shonim shono achar shono**—"And there was a famine in the Days of David for three years, year after year." [1]

We have also experienced three years of famine. Not a famine of bodily sustenance; no, no hunger for bread stalks the streets of our cities. Wartime limitations have not banished the basic necessities of life from our midst. But we have had a spiritual famine for these past three years. Gone from our hearts is the blissful security inspired by a country at peace. We are famished for a return of normal, everyday living; we are hungry for a revival of that tranquillity and friendly relationship between the inhabitants of this globe. We are thirsty for the knowledge of the safety and well-being of our absent loved ones.

---

1. Samuel, II, 21, 1.

The Prophet of antiquity foresaw the coming of such times when he clearly visualized:

"Behold days are coming, sayeth the Lord, when I will send a famine in the land, not a famine for bread, not a thirst for water, but to hear the Words of the Lord."[2]

In our text we find that when Israel suffered that famine in the time of King David, the annointed ruler of our ancestors did not satisfy himself with complaints and woeful lamentations. Indeed we read: **Vayvakesh dovid eth p'nei hashem**—"And David sought the presence of the Lord."[3]

He was anxious to learn the cause of the Divine punishment and sought to irradicate the very causes that occasioned such bitter consequences. We must do likewise if we expect to find material plenty and spiritual contentment in the days ahead. We must seek the Presence of the Lord and search in our hearts to uproot the evil practices, to eliminate the baneful tendencies that cause fractious disputes and discard in our dealings with our fellowmen.

The answer given to David and the Talmudic interpretation placed upon the entire train of circumstance, bears so heavily upon our own problems and reflects so vividly our own shortcomings, that a minute examination of that answer is essential if we are to find our own solutions.

"And he said, 'On account of Saul and on account of the house of blood is this.' "[4]

The years of unhappiness and privation were imposed

---

2. Amos VII, 11.
3. Samuel II.
4. Ibid.

4

upon that generation for many reasons. One reason is given that

"Saul and Jonathan were not properly eulogized."[5]

II

Israel's first crowned king may have fallen from Divine Grace but he died the death of a hero, battling his people's hereditary foes. The bitter anguish of his martyrdom found its climax on the field of honor. In the ecstacy and jubiation that accompanied David's elevation to the throne, the honors that Saul had justly and richly earned were inadvertently omitted. The meaning of the words just quoted is more apparent than a cursory glance reveals. A eulogy properly defined serves a twofold purpose of honoring the departed one and inspiring those who are living. **Aagro d' hespdeo diluio.**[6]

Our Sages no doubt referred to this double significance contained in an appropriate necrology when they assigned the causes for that generation's sorrow. If the Rabbis traced the cause of the disaster to the prevailing negligence toward the memory of fallen heroes, surely in our time, we are justly guilty of similar callousness. On the third wartime Yiskor, our own honored dead, our departed ones whom we recall into our consciousness, the absent hearts whom we remember in fleeting moments, are not really revered. They are improperly eulogized at best, and if our notions are a criteria, they are far from immortalized in our daily lives. They too are: **Nispdu shelo kahalocho.**

We can understand more fully the impact of that historic parallel if we follow the difficulties of King David as

---

5. Talmud, Yebomoth 78b.
6. Talmud Brochoth 6b.

he sought to unravel the mystery and comprehend the cause for his nation's misfortune. In the first year of the famine, the Princely Poet reasoned:

"Peradventure there were in the ranks of Israel those who worshipped on the shrines of strange gods."[7]

As we probe into the reasons that guide the course of human events, we smugly say to ourselves, "Surely the severe chastisement of our time could not be the visitation for such abominable deprivation." The Rabbi is not so certain. He is haunted by the feeling that many in his flock are guilty of just such a transgression. To this Yiskor Service have come people who by all appearances seek to honor the memory of their sainted parents. However, their own personal lives are so radically different from the lives of the people they attempt to honor— indeed, what if every one would be asked directly this list of questions: "Are your ideas and ideals the same as those which motivated the lives of your forebears? Are your Shabbosim kept as theirs were? Are you inspired by the same Festive observances? Are your spiritually bereft existences comparable to their fully integrated religious lives?" The answers to these questions would prove my point. Many of our people do not realize that they are worshipping at a different shrine from that of their parents. They do not realize that a mere memorial and recitation of the sanctified Kaddish is by religious standards akin to idolatrous practice, since everything that is sacred in Jewish Life, on which these prayers are based, are crowded by them into a few standardized stolen moments from their secular pursuits.

To light your Mother's candlesticks on Friday evening, to worship in your Father's Talis and Tephillim every weekday morning, would be a more sincere and honest

---

7. Talmud Yebomoth.

expression of your undying love and respect for your parents, and would be an immensely more effective memorial than the mournful chant of a thousand dirges.

III

King David was not satisfied with only one reason for the famine, but he sought others. As the famine continued to take its toll, he desperately grieved:

> "Perchance there are those who transgress the Laws of God amongst us."[8]

So it is with us in the present day. Of the many transgressions and iniquities for which we must seek forgiveness on this Day of Attonement, none can compare in severity with those sins of omission and commission that our Sages call: **Averoth sheben odom l'chaveroh**— "When we wrong our fellowmen."[9]

These may be the wrongs against individuals and even in a larger sense against the social order of which we are a part. It is thus when eulogies are so painfully inadequate. We mourn only too lightly those who gave their lives so that our country may continue as a bastion of freedom. We cannot pay our obligations to the heroes of Tarawa and Guadalcanal, to the brave men who went to their deaths at Kassarine Pass and at bloody Cassino; we cannot repay these obligations with impressive Honor Rolls and flowery verbal tributes. To honor them in substance would mean that we must honor the cause for which they fell. We should guard for them, since they cannot do it themselves any longer, the ramparts of the Democracy that is uniquely American. God will surely

---

8. Ibid.
9. Talmud, Yumo 85b.

never forgive us this time if we fail once more to keep faith with those who sleep before their time bcause they tried to preserve that faith.

In these trying, transitional days, we need to display a quenchless determination and an unflinching resolve to safeguard unsullied their legacy of freedom; to honor them fully will require that we, in full measure, care for those who are left bereft, gather our energies to comfort the grief-stricken widow and orphan, and build with our utmost efforts, a world that will preclude the possibility of a repetition of these harrowing days. This, above all, will be a task not to be dismissed lightly. We will be faithless to their sainted memories if we fail to bend every effort toward the achievement of the devoted ideal of world peace. This obligation imposed upon us is rendered all the more difficult because the attainment calls for battling two foes, not only those from without, but also those forces of entrenched social reaction in our midst, those sinister voices of chauvinistic nationalists who are already at work seeking to engulf within their prisoned tentacles the soul of American Public Opinion.

IV

Lastly, King David, in speaking as the conscience of his people inquired: **Shemo poskei tzdokoh yesh bochem.**[10] No doubt there are many in our very midst who like the sinners of that period failed to give their adequate share toward the support of the poor and the orphaned, the widowed and the sick. All our sobbing laments and profuse tears will not memorialize our people's martyrs who were the first victims of the present world conflagration. Our Yiskor will be lacking in completeness unless we reinforce it with diligent activities to rescue and rehabilitate those of their kin who are still within the reach of merciful salvation. This threefold significance of this third wartime Yiskor must be understood and implemented in our lives if we care to continue to hallow the ideals which our people respected in the proud and heroic days of Jewish history. To achieve this we must return to worship at the shrine of our forebears, assume our full measure of responsibility in the tasks of reconstruction, and utilize our finest energies in salvaging the remnants of our own people from the black waters of despair which have engulfed them. As we will thus remove the sources of spiritual infection causing tragedy and disaster we can hopefully pray that the scourge of famine be removed from our midst and the blessings of plenty be with us.

Amen

---

10. Talmud Yebomoth.

BEAUTIFUL THOUGH INCOMPLETE*

Preached on the first day of Sukkos, 5704

IN discussing the symbolism of the Festive Booth or Sukkah, we can see that its significance extends to every phase of our lives and to every experience which confronts the Jew.

In its simplest manifestations, the Sukkah represents a temporary structure, a frail hut, which at best will give no appearance of permanence or durability. In this fragile abode, our Sages recognize the dramatization of Israel's martyred history, frail and uncertain, weak and transitory. The average mind would see little of value, in a realistic sense, of such a Sukka-like existance. In viewing Jewish life without the deep philosophical insight contained in the long range historical view, one would see little need for the continued Jewish steadfastness and devotion to the traditions of our people.

The impression of a hasty judgment would indeed be one of pessimistic resignation:

"In my hurried judgment, I concluded that all man is falsehood, vain and hopeless",[1]

but more profound meditation and another chapter will reveal the admission that:

"How can I return unto the Lord even a fragment of His Kindness toward me?"[2]

---

* Reprinted from the Rabbinical Council Manual, 1944.
1. Psalm 116, 11.
2. Ibid: 12.

A better understanding of our own little Tabernacle will reveal the reassuring fact that it serves as a reminder that life must not be full of accomplished blessings in order to be glorious.

II

One of the most impressive ceremonies connected with the observance of the Feast of Tabernacles was the ritual of the ablutions of water over the Festive offering. This sacred ritual was accompanied with much pomp and glory. The Sages of the Talmud speak in descriptive phraseology of the cheering multitude, the chanting Levites, the dancing worshippers, the illuminated torches carried by the participants, and the impressive spectacle of the Kohanim dressed in their sacred vestments. Though the actual ceremony itself consisted of the simple act of pouring water over the sacrificial offering, the genius of our forebears invested this seemingly commonplace observance with glory and splendour. Their religious inspiration and spiritual intoxication lifted them up to the heights of ecstacy, by wrapping in symbolic sanctity their own fate and destiny. It was the Jewish way of expressing the timeless truth that one can find cause for exaltation even in matters of everyday significance. The real joy is to see happy omens in every small manifestation in our daily lives. A people can be genuinely happy only if it rejoices in each manifestation of the Divine Will, though one may not recognize the Divine Will in its everyday hue.

Our Sages very wisely commented: **Mi shelo rooh simchas beis hashoavoh**—"Only he can see real joy in life who is able to detect sparks of sanctity in the simple ceremony of the ablutions of water".[3]

3. Talmud Sukkal, 51b.

A people can be sure of its destiny only if it learns to make peace with adversity and accept cheerfully the commonplace together with the superlative. The Jew hounded and harassed as he was, found joy and happiness in his weak and battered Sukkah, the symbol of his Galuth from without, but which nevertheless enabled him to see the warming glow of the heavenly luminaries as within its walls he peered with anxious eyes toward the starry vault above. As our Yomtov Booth appears uplifting though incomplete, so does Jewish life impress us with its permanence and worthiness in spite of its shortcomings and limitations.

We recall the story of Job and a remarkable statement with reference to his attitude toward life and its manifestations. In more ways than one, Job epitomized the life of the Jew. He too went from golden days to those of deep distress, from power and prestige to complete insignificance, from fabulous fortune to abject poverty. He had to learn from the Jewish way of life to accept a partial realization of his fondest hopes, and do so gracefully At first it appeared to him that without fame and fortune, life was not worthy of the struggle. But when he looked at his fellows, and saw their exaltation in a frail and shaky Booth, it dawned upon him that even just a fleeting ray of sunshine that struggled through the dense foliage into the sukka was worthy of his admiration. He learned that though a Sukka lacks completeness, what it does have is acceptable and useful. One does not always possess the four sides to make his dreams complete. The Jew has the deathless philosophy that dreams and aspirations are in themselves worthy, whether they are ever fulfilld or not. "Kivon sheshoma eyov shesukkoh shel sholos defanoth kesheroh. Miyad niskarroh Daato."[4]

---

4. Yalkut Eliezer, Aleph.

Job watched the frail structure which bent to the elements and trembled in the storm, but which did not break no matter what the circumstances. He then realized that tender sentiments are stronger than the primeval forces, that sensitive feeling outweighs coarse strength, and that the faint murmurs of a sorely tried soul outlast in effect the coarse mouthings of uncouth lips.

The brutal bestiality of German banditry crushed the last waning embers of life in Eastern Europe, but the picture of the haunted Ghetto Jew of Warsaw who pitted the ebbing strength of his emaciated body and the inflamed spirit of his scarred and seared soul against the devastating might of his murderers, will live enshrined in the hearts of sensitive men long after their tormentors are blotted out from the memory of man.

Job found soothing solace to his gnawing questions when he considered that a Little Sukkah was acceptable in the eyes of the Lord, though it was swayed by lashing wind and blinding gale, incomplete and circumspect, still it is the Festive Booth. Its shadows are superior to its sunbeams, but it is still the sign of hope and a symbol of salvation.

Those of us who have drunk in our time the brimming cup of sorrow as we watched the wretched slaughter and sacrifice of the millions of our co-religionists, those of us whose lives have been disordered and upset by the upsurge of overwhelming events, know that our homes are incomplete, that our Sukkah is lacking in more than just one side. Nevertheless, we are firm in our faith and strong in our hope that this humble Sukkah will bring the eagerly desired warmth of light into our lives and sunshine into our midst, when all the world, all the peoples of the earth grasp the meaning of Peace contained in our Tabernacle and the words of the Prophet will come true:

"And all the nations shall go up and worship the King, the Lord of Hosts, and to keep the Feast of Tabernacles"[5]

the stone rejected by the builders will become the cornerstone[6] of a new faith in humanity, a new order of mankind, and a new day for the world which will witness the reestablishment and the strengthening of our falling Sukkah, and Humankind will glimpse and perhaps hold forever, the glory and happiness of peace.

---

5. Zech XIV:10.
6. Psalm 118:22.

THE GOODLY FRUIT OF OUR LIVES

Preached on the Second Day of Sukkos, 5705

WE have been accustomed to the mournful dirge that
wails over the fact that in each passing generation
there is a weakening of traditional ties, and with
each new year there comes a slackening of Jewish interest, and that each new period is marked by the steady
deterioration of our religious standards.

Many observers take it for granted that the children
born to immigrant parents should be less devoted to their
religion than were their forebears. If we examine even
briefly the customs and traditions of our current festive
season, we will readily perceive the fallacy of this attitude. The manifold observances of the Sukkos Festival
always served as an excellent means whereby practical
instruction to our young ones was imparted. The proud
boast of Moses that "With our young and our old shall
we go",[1] was especially evident at this holiday season.
Even the youngest members of the family in days gone
by, anxiously anticipated the construction of the Festive
Booth, and much of the decorative effect in the Tabernacle was a special accomplishment of the younger members of the family. The saintly tradition of placing into
tender hands the coveted **Arbo minim** has given a particular flavor to the significant rituals of the Festival
Booths.

Even in our own greatly curtailed and sadly circumscribed religious endeavors, the holiday of Simchas Torah,
which brings ecstatic climax to the holiday season, ob-
tains most of its joyous accents because of the lively

---

1. Exodus 10, 9.

share and cheerful portion assumed by our youngsters in
the proceedings of that day.

The Biblical command that speaks of another significant holiday observance reads:

> "And Ye shall take you on the first day, the fruit of
> goodly trees . . ."[2]

Our Sages of the Talmud in their anxiety to define properly this holiday ritual, employed a symbolic term which
if profoundly understood will greatly strengthen the
theme of our sermon.   The finest description and closest
definition that they gave us in portraying this goodly
fruit, spoke of a unique characteristic: **K'tanim boim
vadayin g'dolim koyomin.**

> "The little blossoms of the new fruit sprout while
> their predecessors are still on the tree." [3]

Surely the lesson imparted therein is clear, that our aim
must be concentrated on the objective of bringing other
new fruit of our own lives, the young and tender blossoms upon the perennially blooming **Eitz chayim** of Jewish Life, into the House of God: **Vadayin g'dolim koyomin,**
while their parents are in the full glory of their own
Jewish Life.

If only this special aspect of the Sukkos ritual would
provide the pattern for an integrated Jewish Life har-
monizing the past and the present, we would be able to
rid ourselves of the depressing notions that our Synagogues are merely places of refuge for the old type Jew
who glides through the melancholy days of his last years,
or houses the young people only when the traditional
Kadish and other memorial observances are recited.

------

2. Leviticus 23, 40.
3. Talmud Sukkah 35a.

II

The prophetic portion assigned for this morning quotes the inspiring spectacle of King Solomon's prayer when he completed the Tabernacle of God. In his saintly words there abides tender solicitude, reverent homage, and boundless devotion, for the inspiration engendered by his illustrious father David, King of the Hebrews.

> "And he said, Blessed be the Lord, the God of Israel, who spoke with his mouth unto David, my father and hath with his hand fulfilled it." [4]

Is not the lesson clear that instead of considering every new generation weaker spiritually than its predecessor, it should be stronger because of the experience of its forebears, and the added knowledge and power of former generations should enable each succeeding one to excel in culture and enrichment. Thus we see that Solomon went further than David, and upon the foundation laid by his illustrious sire, built the Temple for God's Glory.

Sukkos then, my friends, reminds us vividly and urges us to bear in mind, that our religious practices will only then be true to their sanctified purpose when every strata of Jewish Life, and every group therein, will come joyously into the House of Prayer and sing exultant praises unto Him Who is the Source of all salvation and the Fountain-Head of all bliss. Who is, Who was, and Who ever will be

A Father Just
In Whom We Trust.

Amen

---

4. I Kings, 8, 15.

SHADOWS AND SUNBEAMS

Preached on the Second Day of Sukkos, 5704

A MERICAN Jewry has just demonstrated its capacity
for greatness in the recently convoked solemn
assembly of the American Jewish Conference. Even
impartial observers commented favorably upon the high
degree of idealism which dominated the sessions and
spoke reverently of the "Mystic Passion" which gripped
the delegates when reference was made to the Holy Land.
The sacred enthusiasm generated throughout the gathering, imbued those present with a sense of the spiritual,
and filled them with a high resolve to act for the homeless
and the helpless segments of our people.

The shocking exhibition of that small and sinister force
in American Jewish Life which sought to confuse the proceedings with venomous discord, has all the more earned
our severe condemnation, since its cynical disregard for
the woes and laments of a tortured people found no sym-
pathetic response in the hearts of those who perpetrated
the schism in the ranks of Israel.

We will gain little by merely denouncing the culprits or
by simply dismissing their nefarious schemes as the
neurotic convulsions of a small segment of American
Jewry that refuses to adjust its thinking to the changing
patterns of historical developments. The tragedy of
their lives that impels them to repeat parrot-like the time-
worn shiboleths and platitudes first heard in the land of
Nazidom is especially disheartening, since it indicates
that people otherwise responsible choose to bury their
obstinate heads in the shifting sands of time without
giving heed to the changing winds of circumstance that
shakes the earth to its very foundations.

(49)

The painful record of the American Jewish Committee reinforced by the more open depredations of the Council for American Judaism, may be new in their current manifestations, but the symptoms reveal that their minds merely suffer from chronic ills that plague humanity everytime when traitorous individuals cheerfully sacrifice their people for the supposed advantages gained by their class. This tendency is not limited to our own ranks. The appeasers in every country, as recent experience has shown, have acted likewise.

The problem as it effects our people is best understood if we recall an oft quoted Talmudic passage that deals with people of similar attitudes.

"In days to come, many of the people unworthy of Devine Grace will ask for another chance to observe the Torah and honor its tenets. They then, will be told to observe the Feast of Tabernacles which was honored by everyone building a Sukkah. As the sun beat down heavily, they kicked their Sukkah and left it." [1]

The moral lesson encased in these strange words is best perceived through the application of an ancient fable which is particularly pertinent to our discussion. The sun and the wind once made a wager; the sun said that he was stronger than the wind, and the wind said that he was the stronger. Just then they saw a man walking up the street, and they decided to prove the point by each trying to remove the man's coat. The wind blew and blew as hard as he could but the harder he blew the more tightly the man drew his coat about him. Then the sun came out and it got warmer and warmer. At first the man just opened his coat, but it wasn't long before the pleasant warm rays of the sun caused the man to remove his coat entirely.

---

1. Talmud Abodah Zara 3a.

My devoted friends, there have been people in the history of man who have retained with admirable tenacity their national characteristics in times of oppression and adversity. The people of Poland point with pride to the inability of the Russian Tzars to crush their spirits through the long history of their subdivision. The Cheks recount with justifiable glory, that twenty generations of Hapsburg Horrors could not dampen their free spirit. The people of the Balkan States remained loyal to their cherished traditions during three centuries of Turkish rule; and one can point to numerous other notable instances where the tyranical oppression of conquerors failed to eradicate from the hearts of the conquered peoples their resistless yearning for freedom.

Our people, however, can point to even more distinguished records of resistance to tyranny. The people referred to above, were at least permitted to remain upon their ancestral soil when in subjugation. Very often they enjoyed the free exercise of their religion and at times even the unhampered use of their ancient tongue. We, however, were made to wander from land to land, were driven from continent to continent in a cruel and heartless manner. Yet the agony of our suffering could never quite drown out the hope welling up in our hearts. Living on an alien soil, leading a precarious existence, frequently employing a foreign tongue as a vehicle for their thoughts, our forebears were still able to enrich the treasure house of the world's learning and to deepen the well springs of culture and civilization. There are certain pre-requisites which are usually associated with nationhood and peopledom. Scripture itself establishes the rules and norms through which the commonly accepted channels of a people's existence and survival is guaranteed.

5

"Everyone after his tongue, after their families, in their nation." [2]

The phenomena of our people's survival was made possible without the elements of both Land and Language which are the common foundations of any national structure. Even in their absence, our people accumulated a precious heritage of spiritual heirlooms that enabled them to place upon the altar of humanity a most magnificent offering. The selection of Israel for the divinely appointed task of serving as a carrier of the seeds of holiness made it possible for Israel to rise to its destiny over and above the requirements so indispensable in the creative crucible of other peoples. **V'romam tonu mikol halshnoth.** [3]

The fierce winds of circumstance and the rising gales of oppression that Jewry suffered through its checkered existence was not to be the ultimate test of its devotion to its inherited ideals. A more severe challenge was contained in the conditions of life where the opportunities were vouchsafed unto our people with little or no restrictions. Clever conquerors from the days of antiquity were clearly aware that conquered peoples yielded more easily, their national characteristics, surrendered their right, and merged readily with the wider streams and superior forces that engulfed them, if induced by blandishments rather than terrorized by chastisements. Already in the early experience of Abraham the tempting offer was extended to surrender his spiritual convictions for ample compensation in material aggrandizement. **Ten li hanefsh v'horchush kach-loch.** [4]

The message contained in the fable goes to the very heart of the issue at hand, and indicates more than an

---

2. Genesis X, 5.
3. Festival Prayer Book.
4. Genesis 14, 21.

endurance contest between raging wind and blazing sun. In the light of our problem it contains the moral lesson that it is a more severe test to remain loyal to one's ideals when the warming glow of a friendly sun seeks to induce one to part with his spiritual garments. When the storms of the times menaced the frail Sukkah of the Jews, they remained steadfast in their faith, and they even hurled the defiant gauntlet to those who believe that blandishing enticements and attractive inducements would influence them to part with the priceless heritage of their religion.

Those, however, who were weakened in spirit, mistakenly believe that the enticing glow of assimilation demands as its price self-abasement and self-denial. Sadly do they imagine that for the blessings of equality proffered, they must immolate themselves in the melting pot of uniformity, little realizing that while a national civilization demands unity of purpose, it certainly encourages diversity of interests.

This is the trial that those professing adherence to the council of American Judaism fail to survive. They unfortunately imagine that the privileges of equal opportunity and political liberalism enjoyed in this blessed land of ours, require a surrender of one's cultural heritage and religious uniqueness. An unbiased reading of American History would convince anyone that adherence to one's traditions does not diminish one's devotion to the pristine principles of Americanism, the warp and woof of which proclaimed unbridled liberty of conscience.

These deluded victims of their own fear, like the characters in the Talmudic story, are unable to demonstrate their fidelity to the Tabernacle in the warm sunshine of equal opportunity. They too kick their Sukkah down because they are intellectually unwilling to synthesize the sunbeams from without with the shadows of the Tabernacle from within. In their delusion and self-deception, they imagine that they must slam the door to the past, shut the gate to the future, in order to hold on to the questionable gains of the present. Their miserable abdication need not be the price of their admission into the sacred precincts of America's free spirit. That spirit is much closer to and can live in more harmonious association with the ancient ideals of Israel, which are so beautifully expressed in the meaning and symbolism of our precious Tabernacle.

MAN, THE UNKNOWING

Preached on Shimini Azerth, 5700
Miami Jewish Orthodox Congregation
Miami, Florida

THE moody spirit of Koheleth which is reflected in the heavy hearts at Yiskor is particularly pregnant with meaning, now, when a new world war has had its beginning with Germany's march on Poland. The lights of the world which were far from being aglow yesterday, flicker even lower today, and mankind once again is in the grasp of a terrifying nightmare come true. The summation of King Solomon's pessimistic resignations are echoed from a million hearts that are marched to slaughter:

"Vanity of vanities, all is in vain." [1]   In vain were our fond dreams of an enlightened humanity, in vain our hopes for a world of peace, in vain our prayers for a system of society which would outlaw war as an instrument of national policy.

Indeed, this morbid indictment is voiced by almost every prophet who has even spoken his heart and concluded in utter resignation that it was a dream that built in the air; vapid castles of peace, floating ephemerally somewhere in the stratosphere. Isaiah speaks his bitter lament in the parable of the person who labored diligently to build a vineyard. He laboriously cleaned the soil, picked it free of rocks, built a fence about: "and he hoped to grow grapes", but to his utter sorrow and complete dismay: "and he grew only sour grapes". [2]   The prophet's lamentation gives feeling to our own personal sense of

---

1. Ecclesiastes 1, 2.

disgust with a world that seems to be unworthy of its blessings and incapable of enjoying its limitless advantages.

To anyone who thinks of our present-day civilization as advanced and of our world views as modern, it would come as a severe shock to learn that mankind has made apparently little or no progress since the beginning of history. The average observer will point with pride to the splendid achievements of modern science, to the unbelievable progress of technological projects, as unchallengeable evidence of man's splendid achievements.

Unless one cares to invite abject ridicule upon his judgment, he will have to grant that we have certainly changed the world about us. The physical conditions of man's living standards have certainly undergone fundamental and basic changes. Instead, we have changed the world for man but we have assuredly failed to change man for the world. Viewing mortal man, stripped of the artificial attributes with which he greedily invests himself, we find him essentially the primordial creature, beast-like in his instincts, carniverous in his desires, ferocious in his hunt, and war-like in his spirit.

God has, indeed, regretted having made man for this earth, with his earthly cravings and physical desires. He certainly is not the idealistic creature King David envisioned when he assured us that: "Thou has made him but little less than God." [3] Indeed, man with his capacities to learn, with his ability to adapt himself, with the divine spark in his soul, could have, nay, should have risen to the highest point of ethical perfection and would thus have approximated the dream of David. Instead Man's

---

2. Isaiah V, 2.
3. Psalm, VIII, 6.

cravings have descended into the dust, and his true evaluation comes much closer to the sorrows of Solomon.

"Generations come and Generations go but the world abideth forever." [4] A renowned Talmudic sage has caught in full this Solomanic spirit of sadness and interpreted a statement of Koheleth in a manner which fully explains this awesome attitude. Upon this epigrammatic verse he comments by saying that it should have been reversed and read as follows: "The world cometh and the world goeth but the generations of man remain ever static." [5] In the seemingly meaningless change in the Biblical Verse, we have the true reflection of two diametrically opposed world views. Two attitudes, two evaluations of life and the two summations of Man's own civilization are shown in the two following presentations of the sentence just quoted.

There are those people who maintain that man has registered wonderful gains in his time, they proclaim the remarkable advancement from caveman to scientist; from headhunters to philosophers; from primitive aborigines to intellectual giants. This view is held by those who would believe the Biblical verse in the original form. Generations come and generations go upon the stage of history marking progress and making advancement. Others would side with the sage Rabbi Simon, "The world cometh and the world goeth", the physical appearance of the world is changed. Man may make extensive alterations in his environment: but as for himself, he remains the same, he is stationary in his spiritual gains and, if anything, he has moved backwards. Basically, man today is no better; his methods have changed but his purposes have not. The ends are the same, although the means are clothed in a much more attractive garb. Surely

4. Ecclesiastes I, 3.
5. Ibid., Midrash Rabba.

man has registered brilliant gains in his search to harness for his own good, the limitless sources of nature's blessings. Man has mastered his environment and learned how to make the forces of the universe subject to his will. However, if these brilliant gains were employed exclusively for good and beneficial purposes, then and only then could we exclude that man has changed through the ages and that he has made real progress on this earth. But when the deepest ingenuity of science is employed to construct the means whereby man plots his own destruction and plans his own suicide, then it is difficult to conclude that the human being is the highest in the scale of species.

It would serve us no purpose to belittle the breath-taking achievements of technology, but it would take a long time to convince a mature thinker that the wonderful gains of chemistry are of any useful purpose when scientists are in the employment of the angel of Death; when they turn night into day in their ceaseless search for more deadly gases that would guarantee to wipe out whole cities in the space of a few moments.

"What indeed profiteth man in all his labors, that he labors under the sun?"[6] Should he turn his extensive knowledge, his increasing intelligence exclusively for the good, then his inventions and discoveries would be a blessing and man's ingenuity a source of joy to all.

In the first chapters of Genesis, in the thrilling story of the first man, we read that God instructed him to enjoy and eat all the fruits of the lovely Garden of Eden, with one exception. Perhaps this serves as a symbolic message to humanity to taste all the legitimate joys of the Universe, but with a cardinal exception with one strict prohibition, with a singular severe warning.

---

6. Ecclesiastes I, 3.

"And the Tree of Knowledge, good and bad, ye shall not eat."[7] Perhaps, if the tree of knowledge were to be used for the good values, if man employed the fruits of his knowledge solely for the betterment of humanity and not for evil, then it would not become displeasing to Almighty and fall into the category of "prohibited pleasures".

If science produced only beneficial results, it would be a wonderful boon to humanity and would be God's chosen instrument. But when science struggles to save human lives in danger, and still develops instruments that would destroy men by the thousands, it is a fruit of the Tree of Knowledge which has results both "good and bad", so God wants no part of it and prohibits unto man its enjoyment. Such knowledge if gained, would result in more pain than joy, in more hurt than happiness, and the more we gain by it, the more is the ultimate pain to be.

The increase of such knowledge is sure to increase our woes. Yet even this dreary document, this severe indictment, becomes lightened of its burden if we but turn our hearts to the final warning of Koheleth:

"When all has been said and everything has been listened to, there remains but one supreme task: if we will fear God and obey His Commandments, then we will produce the type of individual who will be all that men consider praiseworthy and beloved."[8]

---

7. Genesis II, 17.
8. Ecclesiastes XII, verse 13.

IN ORDER OF THEIR EMINENCE

A Sermon for Shabbos Chanukah, preached at
Sons of Abraham Synagogue—Kislev 25, 5704
By
RABBI ABRAHAM A. KELLNER

IN DISCUSSING the laws that regulate the kindling of the Chanukah lights, the academies of Shammai and Hillel continued their renowned debates, the former school of thought advocating that the number of the candles must be lit in decreasing order; the latter maintaining that they should be lit in increasing order. Into this seemingly limited range of discussion enters the vast picture of two schools of thought, two divergent philosophies, two sets of attitude with regard to the evaluation of man, his place in the Sun, and his accomplishments for the betterment and ennoblement of the human race. The house of Shammai indeed maintains that Man began his career on the earth most auspiciously, but that he failed to grow in stature or to enhance his position on the ladder of spiritual assent. Its summation about man's place in the purpose of creation is one of philosophic resignation and pessimistic despair. Succinctly it informs us—

"It had been better for man not to be created at all".

An entirely different view is held by the school of Hillel, who considers man still at the starting point in his journey toward his ultimate goal. His spiritual circumstance is indeed frail and humble, and perhaps he is not invested with too many praiseworthy attributes. His growth is hindered though not completely impeded. In the estimation of Hillel, Man lights his candles beginning with one, and adding one more each day as a living symbol of his continuous advancement toward the highest pinnacle of spiritual and intellectual perfection which is represented by the shining lights of the Chanukah Candles.

The whole wide sweep of scriptural literature supports Hillel's contention, and builds a strong case for this school of thought which glorifies a humble beginning and an increasing glory. King David furtively inquires—

> "Who will ascend unto the mountain of the Lord?"[1],
> indicating thereby that man is still at the foot of the mountain, peering upward with anxious eyes, and preparing to dedicate himself to Life's great task of aiming upward, reaching skyward, and groping Godward. In the mature wisdom of Solomon the question is not even asked but the lesson is wisely imparted—
> "The Path of Life leadeth upward for the Intelligent."[2]

The wise men of the Midrash caught the spirit of this significant divergence in the approach to life and its evaluation, and they pointed to important characters of the Bible, who, during their lives, represented these diametrically opposed avenues to salvation. The wise men speak of Moses as a higher and more endearing character than Noah because Moses was first introduced to society at large at the wall of Midyan where he assisted the harrassed daughters of Jethro. Judging by his clothes and appearance, he was spoken of as "Ish Mitzri".

"A man of Egypt",[3] hardly a compliment, one may surmise, in the light of Egypt's slave-holding policy and exploitation; but when last spoken of, in Holy Writ, he is pictured as an "Ish Elochim", "A man of God disbursing Blessings". What a wonderful road was traversed by

---

1. Psalms 24, 3.
2. Proverbs 15, 24.

the man who arose from the status of a lowly shepherd to the postion of divine inspiration. Noah, on the other hand, appears on the stage of history in the full splendor and the royal glory of being the only man who was worthy of salvation in an age of debauchery and degeneracy. The Bible speaks of his as "A righteous man who walks with God", but when Noah takes his leave of this earth, he is described in his declining years as "A man of the earth"[4] who plants a vineyard and degrades himself in the words of the commentator—by disporting himself in drunken stupor before his own offspring. What a tragic fall from the grace of heaven to the disgrace of the earth! **Choviv moshe menoach, noach mishenikroh ish tzadik nikro ish hoadomo avol moshe mishenikroh ish mitzri nikro ish elohim.**[5]

There are many in our midst today who view our bleeding world with the skeptical distrust of the house of Shammai; gloomily do they assert that humanity is sliding steadily downward because of man's inability and unwillingness to challenge his finest energies, deepest sentiments, and highest aspirations toward the elimination of iniquities of society and the inequities of our social order. They see in the terrifying holocaust of this war for survival merely another expression of the madness and lust for power that everlastingly divides humanity into the categories of the oppressor and the oppressed. This group foresees the speedy enthronement of Spengler's dismal prophecies, and it interprets Shammai's law of the decreasing order of lights as an indication that the light of the world is on the decline, and that the hope of humanity lessens with each passing generation.

The school of Hillel, which was ever ready to champion Israel and humanity, establishes a different set of rules.

---

3. Exodus 2, 19.
4. Genesis 9, 20.
5. Yalkut Noach 9.

It accentuates the spiritual growth of man, and it attunes our souls to the hope that though humanity is bereft of the treasure of light, it does possess a humble start, and will in the ultimate increase it, enhance it, and improve it. The school of Hillel proves that light vanquishes darkness, that the soul is stronger than the body, and that the establishment of the supremacy of reason will win over the brutalizing force of unreasoning dictatorship. Just as on that ancient Chanukah, the victory of Hebraic saintliness over sensuous Hellinism reestablished the hope of the Spirit, so must we in our time, though faced with problems of enormous extent and with discouraging experiences, rekindle the lights that will dispel the darkness of despair surrounding us.

The Chanukah Story in its sublimest essence is expressed in the incident of the one vial, of undefiled oil, which kept the flame of our holy Temple aglow until all the lights of that sacred edifice could be kindled anew in their fullest glory and beauty. The world situation, complex as it appears, in the manifold manifestations of human experience, presents a similar situation. The pain and pang that accompanies freedom's rebirth is best understood in the modern application of the above quoted historical experience.

When the darkness of the present world-upheaval extinguished one by one the lights that kept our hopes aflame, there remained one light as in ancient times, which was kept undefiled by impure hands and unprofaned by degenerate fingers. It was the light of the Torah which continued to be aglow, though our Yeshivas had to be transplanted from land to land and from continent to continent, paralleling Israel's wandering through the world. As per the instructions of Hillel, new lights are continually added, lit by the generous heart of the Jews-of-America, in its response to the appeals for overseas

needs. One of these is the light that shines from the
rebuilt communities of our ancient holy land, the light
that was kindled before the liberation of North Africa
and its subjugated peoples. This and other lights are
dear in the sight of God, for they show that the trembling
fingers of man can still strike the fire that will bring
life and hope into the darkest recesses of Man's broken
heart. **Chavvim olay neroth sheaharon madlik min
hamoroth shekovati bashomayim.**[6]

Our Sages in the Midrash Tanehumah were aware of
the lasting value of lights kindled by the quenchless
optimism and boundless enthusiasm of man, for they tell
us, "In the sight of God and in the judgment of the
Almighty, the candles lit by man and the lights emblazoned by the lovers of liberty and advocates of justice,
have a more endearing value and are possessed of more
enduring characteristics than the great and vast luminaries which were hung by Divine command in the trace-
less mystery of the skies. The sun and the moon and the
stars shed their light, spread their warmth, and send
their rays through the length and breadth of the Universe, but greater than even their light, stronger than
even their warmth, and richer than even their brilliance
is the everlasting glory established by the dreamers of
the new and good life here on earth, the dreamers who
light the flaming candles that will disinherit the darkness
shadowing the world today.

---

6. Tanechuma, Tetzave.

THE PASSOVER IDEAL OF FREEDOM

Preached on the First Day of Passover, 5704

I

IT IS timely and fashionable to speak today of freedom and liberation. The Jew, especially, who has been so sorely oppressed throughout the continent of Europe, awaits most anxiously the call to freedom. Yet, gnawing doubt and depressing uncertainty assail many careful observers as they see the pattern of salvation presented in recent months.

A careful reading of today's Scriptural Selection will give us the clue which, if employed, could very properly serve as an example that leaders of mankind might profitably follow. This Biblical Portion depicts the minutiae of the Passover sacrifice, a ritual which preceded the departure of our ancestors from the land of their tormentors. The first suggestion readily evident is that freedom will not be obtained except at the cost of a sacrifice. Furthermore, Holy Writ warns: "And it shall come to pass when ye come to the land which the Lord will give you, that ye shall **KEEP** this service."[1] The important lesson thereby imparted is that liberty once attained must be carefully guarded. The "Eternal Vigilance" of which our patriotic forefathers spoke has its roots in the Holy Writ in this quotation which admonished us that sacrifices for the Freedom Ideal must continue even when a people are seemingly, safely ensconced on their own soil.

---

1. Exodus 12, 25.

(65)

II

Next in importance is the understanding that liberation as construed by Moses envisaged man free from physical and spiritual slavery. The very first statement foretelling Israel's eventual salvation established this principle by declaring in clear accents:

> "When thou has brought forth the people from Egypt, they shall serve God upon this mountain."[2]

Very emphatically then was the policy here enunciated that Israel's freedom will go hand in hand with the acceptance of the Divine Law; in the pithy summation of the Mishna:

> "A man is only free when he engages himself in the study of the Divine Law".[3]

When our forefathers departed from Egypt, thus ridding themselves of physical slavery, they could not as yet enter the promised Land. Though the distance should have been traversed in a rather short time, it took them forty tortuous years to span the Arabian Desert because they were unprepared for Spiritual Freedom. Surely they thought themselves ready to take possession of the soil, but the Psalmist tell us: **E'hem lo yodu drochoi.**

> "They as yet knew not My ways."[4]

Theirs was the task of ridding themselves of the impurities of the mind and the soul acquired through contact with idolatry and kindred Egyptian abominations. Our forefathers were allowed to enter the Holy Land when

---

2. Exodus 3, 12.
3. Aboth 6, 2.
4. Psalms 95, 10.

they themselves became holy in spirit and sanctified in purpose. This spiritual motif is emphatically re-stated in the command of Joshua to the people who were about to enter the Land. We read in the opening words of Today's Haftorah:

"And Joshua said unto the people 'Sanctify Yourselves'."[5]

Only when this injunction was followed, and the people maintained their ancestral holding within the realm of Godliness, were they able to enjoy its possession.

The Rabbis of the Midrash followed this thought pattern when they removed the seeming paradox from two contradictory statements in King David's Psalms. They sought to harmonize the conflict between an earlier pronouncement which held:

"The Earth is the Lord's and the fullness thereof,"[6]

with a later statement that told us:

"And the Earth He gave to the children of men".[7]

The difference the Rabbi saw was:

Kan kodem brocho, kan l'achar brocho.[8]

Before a man utters a benediction and acknowledges his gratitude to the Source of all blessings, everything belongs to God, but when man soulfully records his recognition of God's Fatherly care of His children, then the earth and its fullness thereof are here for man's joy and advantage.

Yea, my friends, the untold riches of the world about

---

5. Joshua 3, 5.
6. Psalms 24, 1.
7. Psalms 115, 15.
8. Ibid., Midrash Rabba.

6

us, the undreamed of bliss of a world permanently at
peace, the unrealized goal of a prosperous humanity,
these could all be attained if the primary prerequisites
enumerated about would be honored. If mankind return
to prayer and service, to blessing and understanding, then
all the glories possible in earthly existence would be
vouchsafed unto us by a Benevolent Providence.

Humanity was plunged into this war and the world
turned it into a shambles because the only consideration
of the people was land, and the only concern of Government was territory. A tyrannical dictatorship clamoring
for more and more "Lebensraum" ran roughshod over
peoples and their possessions, caring very little for right,
justice, or human decency. Israel, on the other hand,
had in times of olden, set the classic example, that in days
of spiritual self-sufficiency, earthly considerations rank
little if at all. Thus we are told that when countless
thousands thronged the Temple Courts in those golden
days in Jerusalem to share in the magnificent glory of the
Divine Service, never was there a demand heard for more
"Lebensraum" for none ever said: **"Tzar li homokom."**[9]

III

Now when the world is moving steadily closer to liberation, we must take stock and see whether the spiritual
ingredients so necessary for the survival of our hopes
enter into the plan of those who want to translate the
victory of our arms into the triumphant march of
humanity. All of our sacrifices would be in vain, all of
our efforts spent for naught, if **our** sole concern too, will
be with division of land, control of territory, and maintenance of possessions. What would it profit humanity
to change the landscape of the world if man should re-

---

9. Aboth 5, 7.

main ever the same—unimproved and without idealism.
How poignantly did Markham sing

> We are all blind until we see
> That in the Human Plan
> Nothing is worth the making
> If it does not make the man.

Unless we can effectively free the minds of men from the
poisons and prejudices, the spitefulness and distrust, and
the hateful predilections, that darken the horizon of
humanity today, all will be in vain.   The poet so lament-
fully continues:

> Why build these cities glorious
> If many unbuilded goes
> In vain we build the world
> Unless the builder also grows.

In vain, said King David ages ago, will the builders labor
unless God helps us to build the house of our hopes.   The
Passover Ideal of Freedom emphasizes the free spirit of
man rather than his freedom to extend his holdings, expand his territory, and enlarge his possessions.   Man's
darkened vision, his narrowed ideals, his circumscribed
outlook, must be mended from within, before we can proceed to repair his bleeding world from without.

This in brief is the ways of our ancient Passover which
would adequately serve if invoked the problems of our
modern Egypts.   It speaks not only to the vanquished
enemy who caused oceans of blood and torrents of tears
to be unloosed upon humanity, but also to some of the
potential victors who seemingly learned little from the
five years of blood and sweat and tears.   Those who still
think in terms of "Balance of Power", "Spheres of Influence," "Lifeline of the Empire", and the like, ought to
turn with the humility born of suffering to the deathless

story of Passover which insisted on the liberation of **man** as the first essential step in the liberty of the world.

We are all familiar with a little story currently popular. It tells of a man who was enjoying his Sunday comfort by reading his newspapers and magazines. He was continually disturbed by his little son who asked him question after question. Becoming annoyed, he tore the cover-page from his magazine into very small pieces and said to his boy, "Here my son, I tore up this map of the world. You go up to your room and paste it correctly together. If and when you put it together correctly, you can come down and ask me any question you please and as many as you like." The little boy acted accordingly and very shortly returned to his father with the map put together perfectly. In amazement and consternation his daddy asked him how he had succeeded in such a difficult task in such a short time. "It was very simple," said the little fellow. "On the other side of the map was a picture of a man. I put the man together and the map came out all right." Yes, my friends, the task of the world today is to put **man** together, place hope in his heart, music on his lips, enlarge his vision and extend his spirit, and the world will blossom forth like the Garden of the Lord on the day of Creation.

THE PASSOVER GUARANTEE OF
FREEDOM

Preached on the Second Day of Passover, 5704

YESTERDAY'S sermon developed the main trend of the Passover Freedom Ideal, and this morning I will attempt to delineate the theme that the enchanting refrains of Exodus in those days can still be music to our ears and sweet song to our souls.

If judged by surface indications alone, there will be little to rejoice about at the current Passover Festival; indeed, the Guarantee of Freedom is conspicuous by its absence, throughout most of the world. In a state of darkness, when the sun of Freedom goes down, only a hardy spirit like that of King David can stand firm and stoutly proclaim his faith supreme **Vemunoscho balelos**[1] although the shadows of the night envelop man and terrify him with a thousand images of haunting horror. Indeed one poet felt that nothing, that the blue coolness of an evening sky decorated by the starry vault above, could offer would compensate one for the loss of the brightness of the day when the dazzling radiance of the sun sheds its cheerful rays.

> The Night has a thousand eyes
> And the day but one
> Yet the light of the whole world dies
> With the dying sun.

One can trace this fearsome distrust to the early days of creation when Adam first was confronted with it as the terror of the night settled over his head and the lurking

---

1. Psalms 92, 3.

(71)

shadows brought a fear of unknown horrors to his primitive conscience.

Though the languor of the moon has been toasted in song and story and the dazzle of scintillating stardust rhapsodized by countless poets, the night is still considered by many as the harbinger of evil. In fact, the Talmudic Sages comment: **V'lachoshech koro loyloh**— "And the Darkness He called Night".[2] Suggestion here is made, they thought, of the darkened machinations of wicked men. **Ilu maasehem shel r'shoim.**

It is small wonder then that even profound observers find little to rejoice about, in the shadowy days of Jewish existence. Their reactions were best expressed by the lamentful longing of those who wept on the banks of the rivers of Babylon, "For how can I sing the songs of the Lord in a strange land?"[3] To these critics the observance of a Freedom Festival in times of renewed slavery is incongruous, many indeed go further and consider it a cruel joke, a ghastly jest played upon the heart-strings of a romantic and incurably sentimental people. A similar perplexity, if not a final conclusion, assailed the fine mind and noble character of Rabbi Elazar Ben Azarya who was called to leadership in a similarly critical epoch and who was endowed with learning and wisdom much beyond his years. Yet for the philosophical outlook that one acquires through the experience of years, he turned to a distinguished colleague. In his own mind he was deeply perturbed and anxiously queried: **V'lo zochisi shetomar yetzias mitzraim balelos**—"I could not understand and never grasp", he opined, "how one can rejoice and jubilantly recount the Passover Story when the darkness of the night is characteristic of this age."[4]

---

2. Genesis 1, 5.
3. Psalm 137, 4.
4. Talmud B'rochoth 12b.

It seemed to him incomparable with the horrors of Roman occupation endured in his day that people should exult over a past liberation. It seemed difficult to burst into song when the only other sounds heard in the gloomy present were those caused by the chains as forged by their current tormentors. But along came Ben Zoma, a man given to philosophical evaluations and speculative thinking.[5] Tenderly he reminded Rabbi Elazar that one does not judge history by isolated instances or individual manifestations. One must indeed take into account the whole wide range of the cavalcade of progress if he is to judge the accomplishments and failures of the past and the present. In fact, he must go even further, and look ahead, beyond the rim of the future, and by the totality of the impression thus gained reduce his observations to a mature and distilled judgment. When one reads the Scriptures correctly, he tells us, one should consider **ALL** the days of Israel's existence—**Kol y'mei chayecho.** Any other conclusion would be incomplete and no particular phase of Jewish life is distinct and separate by itself. We must look upon each individual, historical manifestation as a segment of a Divine and designed pattern whose total glow has made an indelible impression upon the footprints of history.

Surely in the days of those Talmudic giants, as in our own day, one can find more to weep for, than to be jubilant about. Those happy experiences that we may find in our present generation become subdued and colorless in the light of the indescribable bestiality and horror experienced by our people in the lands of their sorrows. But Jewish History as a whole—the story of the Jew as told in Kol y'mei recounting **ALL** his days—replaces the sombre color of desolation with the the bright panorama of triumphant achievements. In the Spiritual heavens of our harrassed people, shine countless luminaries whose

---

5. Ibid., 57b.

light no human hand can dim, no mortal man can extinguish. When one remembers the glory of our Prophets, the songs of our Psalmists, the wisdom of our Sages, and the philosophy of Maimonides and numerous others like him, he takes into account the total configuration of Jewish History and must perforce conclude that "Behold, it was good."

Yea, my friends, if we add up the deathless story of our people's wanderings, recount the heroism of our brave martyrs, tell the thrilling tale of pioneers in the Holy Land, probe deeply into the souls of our poets, thinkers, and philosophers who immortalized in song and story the dream of the ages, and if we add to these with pride that our religion and its teachings served as the foundation stone for civilization—the society of which we are part and parcel—, then, and only then, will we appreciate the Guarantee of The Passover Freedom Ideal.

In the light of this interpretation we will readily comprehend why the Jews now celebrate Passover during a night darker even than that of Egypt, in a bondage more than that under the Pharoahs. Should he be enslaved anew, the Jew will, even in a deep dungeon, exultantly proclaim:

"Therefore we are bound to thank, praise, laud, glorify, extol, honor, bless, exult, and reverence Him, Who did all these miracles for our ancestors and for us, for He brought us forth from bondage to freedom, from sorrow to joy, from mourning to Holy Days, from darkness to great light, and from servitude to redemption, and therefore let us sing unto him a new song; HALLELUYAH."

DIVINE GRATITUDE*

Preached in Congregation Petach Tikvah, Baltimore
7th day of Passover, 5696

A S A charming spring song that brings welcome relief
in the wake of the dreary monotony of the winter,
so does the Biblical reading of this morning bring
joyous exultation into our lives, as we are thrilled anew to
the even deathless refrain of the Song of Moses.

This first song of hope and glory affirms tomorrow's
hope even before it acknowledges yesterday's glory. The
emphasis say our Sages is not so much on a recognition of
things past as much as it is on an affirmation of faith in
the songs yet to be sung, the glories yet to be achieved.
Shor lo neemar.[1]

Often overlooked and less fully appreciated is the
accompanying song of Miriam, the Prophetess, which com-
pletes the Biblical recital.

She, too, glorified God, and her majestic accents of
praise should not be dwarfed by the major symphony
which is contained in the song of Israel's greatest master.
Truly Miriam was entitled to supreme exultation, for her
prophetic vision and unconquerable hope shone ever
brightly even in the days of deepest despair. To appreciate in full Miriam's share in the rhapsody of **Oz yoshir**
we must trace our steps backwards and throw the spot-
light of investigation upon a well-known Biblical passage
and its significance in the light of Talmudic interpretation.

---

* Reprinted from the Rabbinical Council Manual, 1943.
1. Talmud, Sanhedrin 91b.

All of us have been moved by the pathetic story of Moses, whose brave mother made heroic attempts to conceal him from the Egyptian oppressors. History records that in the darkest days of the Russian Revolution millions were harassed and massacred in the wake of fratricidal wars and ferocious pogroms. Thousands of our people crouched in the dungeons of dark cellars hoping that they may escape with their lives if they remain unnoticed. Mothers of crying infants placed pillows over weeping mouths lest their cries betray their hiding place. Jocheved perhaps was compelled to employ similar methods to hide the existence of a new child. But when all was of no avail, she proceeded to place the frail child upon the banks of the river Nile, rather than to permit the cruel taskmasters of Pharoah to seize him. But when Moses was placed in the bulrushes, he was not alone. Besides the protecting Presence of Providence, he was watched over by Miriam, who did not surrender her hope in his ultimate rescue and survival.

"And his sister stood from afar."[2]

Miriam was not content to let the child be taken care of by the shifting hands of circumstance. No! She was to stand there to watch what would become of him. What will become of the dreams and hopes that they all had for the future leader? Indeed the word **Merachock** seems at times to indicate the assumption that Miriam looked into the distant future. The prophetess, undaunted by the disappointments of the present, fixed her vision upon a farther horizon and thence sought solace for the sorrows of the moment. She submerged herself in a reverie of dreams, and summoned all the imaginative capacities of her sensitive soul to conjure up a vision of salvation in her moment of misery. Indeed students of Biblical philology interpret **Vatesazav** to mean that "she took

2. Exodus 11:4.

her stand". It is safe to assume that the inference here is that Miriam took her stand for hope in the face of misfortune; that she evinced an unflinching loyalty to her people. She felt sure that the victories of the future will right the wrongs of the present.

Miriam's undaunted courage reaped its dividends not only in the miraculous delivery of Moses but it obtained for her the glories of Godly gratitude, so beautifully related in conjunction with an incident in the latter life of our heroine.

II

Eight decades have passed into the lap of history and Moses is in his prime as the leader and law giver of his people. Miriam is still the devoted and the loyal sister, zealously guarding her brother's material as well as spiritual safety. Suddenly she encourages the wrath of God and suffers in consequence a malady which prevents her from joining the camp of Israel. According to Biblical law, she was to live apart for seven full days, but the Bible relates that the entire multitude remained with her and journeyed not for seven days. Our sages in commenting upon this remarkable incident state that this honor the Omnipresent showed unto her as a reward for her faith, when she tarried for Moses an hour.[3]

"The judgments of the Lord are true righteous altogether".[4]

Often it seems to mortal man that Heavenly reward and Divine gratitude is slow in coming, but herein we behold the most dramatic demonstration of the Almighty's

3. Sotah 10b.
4. Psalm 20:10.

never failing reward unto those who observe His com-
mands and have faith in His judgments. It would be all
out of proportion to assume that a multitude of 600,000
men with their families would be kept from their appointed tasks merely because the Eternal wanted to register His gratitude unto Miriam for the anxious hour of
waiting she bestowed upon her brother. Perhaps one
need not even be compensated for attentions paid to one's
kin. At any rate, the waiting of one hour by one person
does not normally justify the tarrying of an entire nation
for the period of seven times 24 hours.

In the light of our previous discussion, however, this
problem is easily solved. It was not merely concern for
her brother alone that motivated Miriam but concern for
a people whom her brother symbolized; if we understand
that Biblical passage to mean that Miriam surveyed the
tragic plight of the Hebrews and sought to find a source
of salvation for their troubles; if we believe, as we do,
that the prophetess with her waiting encouraged every
heart with hope at a time when even her mother's heart
was crushed in abject sorrow and defeat, then it stands to
reason and it is right that the entire people should tarry
and repay her unyielding trust with a patient wait of
seven days.

In the whole wide sweep of Biblical literature, which
abounds in enraptured expressions of glory and gratitude,
none compares with the majesty and grandeur of
Miriam's hopeful waiting and her rich reward of Divine
Gratitude.

In our times of trials and tribulations, the understanding of such remarkable revelations help us to fasten ourselves to the tried and tested moorings of the past. They
gladden our hearts and strengthen our souls as they
speak of faith divine. In a God divine, and they bring

unto us the reassuring message that the bleak misery of today will be compensated for in the glorious sunshine of tomorrow, when the call of the prophets will be a Heavenly symphony to our ears, a gladdening balsam to our hearts and a soothing healing to our souls.

THE TRIUMPH OVER ADVERSITY

Preached on the last day of Passover, 5703

THE story is told about the sainted Chofetz Chaim that once he was visited by a trusted disciple and in a conversation the visitor was asked how thing in general were with him. With a deep sigh, he answered, that things indeed were bad. The saintly Rabbi then reproved him by saying that surely his situation must be bitter and not bad, and he urged him to accept his fate in that sense. Upon being questioned what the difference between the two could be, his revered master told him, a sick person is often commanded to take a medicine the taste of which is bitter in the extreme. Only a foolish patient would conclude that because of its bitterness, the medicine is bad. Instead he would conclude only the transitory sensation is bitter, but the lasting remedial effects of the potion are indeed very good. Similarly, my son, said the great teacher, we must accept life's difficult experiences as a healing potion whose taste may not be very pleasant, but whose ultimate purposes are only for the good. God, our great Healer, sometimes prescribes a medicine that may be bitter to the extreme, but the righteous person will humbly acknowledge it and seek the ultimate outcome of the Divine Visitation.

This energizing faith which the Chofeitz Chaim aims to convey is certainly the paramount need of our times, and must be brought into play to help abjure the pessimism and banish the hopelessness created by the frightful ravages of global war, and caused by the bestial policy of Horrendous Nazidom.

To seek the spiritual armor with which the steadfast servants of God have ever recognized the ultimate good

(80)

as against the immediate overpowering evil, I will bespeak your attention to the prophetic portion which we read in today's ritual. In this peroration Isaiah envisions the eventual coming of the Redeemer, and he envisages the divinely inspired attributes of leadership exhibited by this Godly Emissary. He will be imbued by the spirit of knowledge and the fear of God, and will in the words of Isaiah: "Judge the poor with righteousness and reprove them with equity for they are the poor of the earth."[1] This theme is emphasized ever and anon and the prophet further elucidates that this Divinely appointed man will have Righteousness and Fidelity, Justice and Faith as his watchwords.

"And Righteousness shall be the girdle of his loins, and Faithfulness the girdle of his reins."[2] Isaiah saw this vision in a dissolute and terrible time akin to that of ours. He thereby taught us the lesson that it is in ominous days that we must catch a glimpse of God's Spirit on earth, and that it is then, in an era of turbulence, that we must strengthen the armor of our Faith. He went a step further and implied that next to transmuting calamity into a firmer faith, we must reduce the strain and tension occasioned by the cruel experiences and stress of the times, and we must do this by the application of **righteousness** and by the practice of **just** deeds—which is the Hebrew idiom for charitable practices.

Paradoxically enough, our Sacred Tongue which is rich in idiomatic expressions and which abounds in synonyms, does not have a term for charity as such. The genius of the Hebrew language expresses the all-important concept that supporting the poor and poverty-stricken, taking care of the needy, and looking after our less fortunate fellow-men is the "Just" thing to do—a true expression of

1. Isaiah. 12, 4.
2. Ibid., 5.

Justice. All the laws of the Bible about alms to the needy, assistance to the homeless, and help to the orphaned and widowed, are the manifestations of the concept of Justice and just dealings. It is not alone with moral axioms that our Torah is concerned; the Torah applies itself concretely to the welfare and happiness of the people, thus cementing the foundations of social order whose explicit aim it is to improve the moral fabric and ethical texture of our civilization.

The prophet dreamed and anticipated the transition from stark terror to peaceful pursuits by means of the twin forces of Faith and Justice. We, too, must leave no stone unturned in our effort in the direction which will redeem some of the sorrow of our seasons by strengthening the faith of those who are swayed by the hammer-blows of history, and by according a just measure of our support to those who are racked by the horror of war and extermination.

These two essential symbols which turn despair into hope were clearly marked in the life of our grandsire, Abraham. He, too, approached the evening of his life with the agony and tears that mark a person who sees disaster in the present and desolation in the future. He saw the tender hopes of his youth shattered as he realized that there was no possibility of transferring to posterity the high hopes and noble purposes which had activated his pilgrimage on this earth. He saw himself passing on to the Great Beyond without kin or heir.

Then came to him the assurance of God that the stars above and the sands below would be the symbols of the untold progeny that would spring from his loins. He looked upon the dazzling stardust as his guiding light, and he heard in the crescendo of the rising and receding waves of the ocean the challenging patterns of Jewish history as it passed from gloom to glory, from the darkness of defeat to the dawning of victory. Logical reasoning and callous calculations would not have impelled such a sweeping change in the Abrahamic outlook. Sublime faith and profound trust in the recompense of Heaven were the props of his support.

"And he believed in God and He accounted it for Righteousness."[3] This devoted loyalty was treasured in Heavenly opinion and highly prized by Divine authority. It was a sublime faith that was the witness of his soul, the invincible armor of his heart. It was a faith that was strong enough to move mountains, to divide oceans, to ride the crest of a hurricane, and to surmount the rumblings of a world-shattering quake. It was the faith that stood in support of his descendants when they cowered at the shore of the stormy sea. "Because of Abraham's stolid faith, the Red Sea parted for his descendants."[4] The historical process through which God revealed Himself unto His children was accepted by Abraham and his posterity with unshaken faith even when it appeared baffling on the surface and distressing in form.

In our time, when it seems that the nightmare of the darkest ages stalks menacingly across the stage of our world, we, too, must be steadied with the defensive weapons of **Emunoh** and **Tzedek** that sustained our illustrious forebear when he faced the mounting tribulations of his times. We, who wander in the valley of sorrows, must be sustained by the strength of faith, and be shown the redemptive qualities of justly applied charity. There are those among us who view with abject resignation the crushing blows dealt to Israel, and discern in the lamentful woe of our martyrs the deathknell of a historic people. They are indeed like the man who suffered a succession of

---

3. Genesis 15, 6.

ailments and maladies; his anguish was so extreme that he gave up all hope of recovery and all interest in life. He continually envisaged his inevitable end, and drove his family frantic by his premonitions and his resignation. To impress upon him his foolishness of attitude, his physician, offered to cut his vein and prove to him that he was very much alive, but even this did not help; the patient merely peered wishfully into the air and remarked "It only proves that the Dead are bleeding."

There are countless numbers of Jews crushed to the ground by the sledge hammer blows of adversity, who look upon the stream of blood flowing from the myriads of wounds inflicted upon our people as blood flowing from the body of a dead people. To these we speak in the words of Ezekiel who saw a pillar of hope rise from a valley of dry bones. He was a prophet of exile who never failed to exhort his people with encouraging perorations, and to strengthen them in the blackest hour of their night of exile. He bespoke Heavenly consolation when he thundered God's assurance.

"And I will pass over thee and see thee wallow in thy blood and I say unto thee, in thy blood shalt thou live, in thy blood shalt thou live."[5] This conviction not only deepens the philosophic content of Judaism, but it also throws out the challenge that it is not the dead that are bleeding but that it is their resurgent sign of life which hallows our existence and enables us to rise to the heights of opportunities provided by the tragic turn of events.

Next to the enthronement of Faith comes the need for Tzdokokoh—Justice and just dealing which will take shape in the form of righteous deeds. The historic privilege of American Jewry has ever been the task of extending a supporting hand to our stricken brethren.

---

5. Ezekiel 16, 6.

This was at all times one of the major notes in the symphony of Jewish life, and it is, indeed, part and parcel of the traditional Passover observances. However, never before were the opportunities so vast, the need so stupendous, the urgency so vital, and the cause so hallowed. In the efforts of our community, we of the Synagogue must participate in a manner most vigorous. Those of us assembled here this morning, who, by their very presence and participation in these Memorial services, demonstrate their unquenchable faith in life after death and in triumph of Light over Darkness, must evince unyielding hope in the unbroken continuity of Jewish life, and help with ever increasing devotion the cause of rehabilitation, relief, and rescue, which is the guiding pattern of salvation. These are the three great agencies united in this joint drive.

The ages bear immutable evidence as to the sanctity of our cause. History will judge us by the effectiveness of our aid brought into play at this critical juncture. The person who weighs his answer will do well to remember that the question at stake is the survival of a whole generation of Jews. Ours is the sacred privilege to help them live again.   Amen.

THE GROWING CONCEPT OF GOD

IN THE sweeping grandeur of the Story of Revelations as it was unfolded in this morning's Biblical narrative, there is a closing observation which has been the cause of countless comments and interpretations. The statement: **V'chol hoom roim eth hakoloth**—"And all the people perceived the Thundering Voices",[1] causes the Sages of the Midrash to speculate on the plural form in which the Recording Voice of the Almighty is represented. Their answer is at once a solution of the perplexities of the query as well as a theological view of the deepest import.

It was One and the Same Voice of God, but it sounded different to each one: each and every individual heard That Voice issuing from the corridors of Eternity: the old heard It according to their strength, the young heard It as per their knowledge. Even Moses heard It according to his own mental powers. **B'kocho shel kol echod voechod.**[2]

In this profound Midrashic homily is established not alone the Jewish **idea of Monotheism,** but also the unique nature and the exalted scope of that idea. We cannot conceive of A Deity Whose Nature is exactly defined or Whose Powers are specifically enumerated. Rather do we try to think of Him in an Imagery of Limitlessness, constantly and steadily growing, expanding, and increasing in our concept. He looms Larger in our consciousness each time we behold the wondrous nature of His Works and the remarkable extent of His Creations.

---

1. Exodus XX, 18.
2. Exodus Rabba V.

Truly God is Unchanging and is ever the Same; only our knowledge of Him expends, but God is His Illimitable Glory Was, Is and ever Will be, as Scripture says.

"Behold and see now that I am ever I."[3]

always and everywhere, ever and at all times God. Only our knowledge and estimate of Him is enhanced with every experience that opens up new vistas before our eyes. Every added manifestation of God's Glorious Majesty, and all occurrences that enable us to pierce the magic mystery of life endowed through Divine Loving Kindness, make us think of Him from Whom all blessings flow in an increasing tempo. Just as the promulgation of the Decalogue was not apparent to all alike, the Words of God spoken to the anxious assemblage encamped beneath the mountain reached everyone in the measure of his own intelligence: and so must our own individual concept grow and expand with the widening powers of our comprehension and with the added degrees of our intelligence.

The order of our daily prayers in the Amidah repeats separately: **Elokei avrohom, elokei yitzchok, v'elokei yaakov**[4] though it would have sufficed to say: **Elokei avrohom—yitzchok v'yaakov**—"The God of Abraham, Isaac, and Jacob"; the specific reference to each one of the ancestors implies also that each succeeding generation has added to its knowledge of God, and that every new-comer upon the stage of our history increases our concept of the Infinite and widens our range of understanding It.

Abraham felt it necessary to institute the morning service in order that he might praise the Name of God with

---

3. Deuteronomy XXXII, 39.
4. Daily Prayer Book.

the rising dawn; his son Isaac went one step beyond—his
spiritual aspirations urged him to establish the Mincha
service with the setting of the sun when the twilight calm
betwixt the day and the night reminds us of the opportunity to commune alone with Our Maker.   Jacob of the
third generation, had inherited the God intoxication from
his forebears and added his own advanced concept woven
from his additional experiences; thus he established the
Maariv or Evening Service, in response to his feeling that
there is need for man to seek his Creator when the
silvery stars of the blue heavens peer out of the moonlit
skies, guarding a sleeping humanity.   King David added
to this all encompassing philosophy when he suggested
that every day of our lives helps us to expand our knowledge of God, and that the daily experiences accruing over
a lifetime aid us in our comprehension of the Divine
Existence that makes us conscious of things spiritual and
Godly.

> "Day unto day uttereth speech and night unto night
> revealeth knowledge."[5]

There is so much in the realm of the mystic in the
world about us, so much of the wondrous and magic in
life's great experience, that each succeeding manifestation of the wonder of life should enrapture our exalted
spirits into a greater belief and a deeper reverence.   A
great doctor once stated that all the scepticism engendered within his soul through the pseudo-scientific
scoffiness of modern agnostics vanished like a shadow
when he operated on a fellow human being for the first
time and saw the remarkable Handiwork of God manifest
in the perfect mechanism of a living man, thus expressing
the thought long ago voiced by Job: **Umivsori echzeh
elokei**—"From my flesh I see evidence of my God."[6]

---

5. Psalms 19, 3.
6. Job 19, 26.

Some of our fellowmen, perhaps hastily, surely foolishly point to the magnificent achievements of modern
discoveries, and want to discredit therewith the powers
of religion. Instead we say that these very inventions
bespeak the Greatness of God and the Justness and the
Magnitude of His Creations. Every atomic power, every
electric current, every resource of nature harnessed by
the ingenuity of man, has been vouchsafed unto us and
for our advantage from the very day of Creation, and has
been patiently deposited in the bosom of the world for
man's comfort and benefit.

The more we find in the realm of nature which will
benefit mankind, the more we find of untold blessings in
the depths of the sea, in the bowels of the earth, and in
the vaults of the Heaven and its vastness—the more we
stand enraptured with awe before the Magnificent Majesty of God's Incomparable Powers. That is why we
think of God, not in terms of static power defined and
limited in scope, but in terms of ever-changing and ever-
expanding Power.

There is a specific command in Scriptures which, if delineated in terms of our erstwhile discussion, clearly
carries the implication that we are prohibited from im-
agining the Almighty in any Given Form, in any Specific
Concept, in any Definite Fashion. In the ten commandments recited before, we heard the injunction against
describing in portrait form or sculpture, or in carving or
painting, the Almighty, Blessed be He. We are told that
He is neither specifically in the Heavens above, on the
earth below, or in the deep ocean. He is in all of these
places all at once and in many, many more places at the
same time. We read of another command in a later
chapter of Exodus where we are told: **Elokei maasecho lo
saase loch**—"Thou shalt not make thyself a molten
God."[7] This repeated emphasis, we believe, was neces-

sary in order to prevent us from envisioning God in any Given Form, in any Specific Mould, or in any Established Pattern. Our must be a fluid rather than a fixed concept, mobile rather than static, growing in magnitude rather than receding in the oft too familiar notion. Our understanding should react with the sensitivity of a most delicate instrument to every occurrence in life, to every new thrill, to every new discovery, to every new opportunity which unfolds before us the spacious firmament on high and all the glories of the handiwork of our Creator.

Every Jewish Festival is characteristic of some observance and contains in its mood the particular nuances of a spirituality which comes to life in the rites and rituals of the Festive Ceremonials. On Shevuoth we recall the experience of a family in the old world whose breadwinner leaves for these shores to seek fame and fortune. He prospers and sends home in a lavish manner the riches he accrues. In spite of the dazzling affluence that is their lot, the family writes letters beseeching the father to return home and live with his family in happy union. They desire the blessed influence of his presence more than the wealth and opulence that could be theirs if he remained on a distant shore.

Thus is shown the significance of Shevuoth; our other holidays abound with more festive colorings and a greater variety of observances. On Passover we enjoy the glorious traditions of the inspiring Seder; our Sukkoth is beautified with flowers and other rich colors of Nature, and we carry with pride the proud Lulab. On the Pentecost holiday we lack all these symbols but we have with us the message that brings near unto our hearts the enduring concept of Our God Who dwells in our midst and in Whose Limitless Powers we glory as we reaffirm today and forever our abiding trust in His Merciful Salvation.

---

7. Exodus XXXIV, 17.

As we send unto Him the glorious rhapsody of our inspired souls, we feel within ourselves the spiritual quality of Halevy's longing cry:

> O Lord where can I find Thee:
> Where is Thy Eternal Resting Place?
> And where can I not find Thee?
> Full of Thy Glory is the infinite space.

MAKE WAY FOR TOMORROW

Preached on the Second Day of Shabuoth at The Miami
Jewish Orthodox Congregation, 5699

THE memorial mood, which prevails on Yiskor morning, is eased somewhat by the consolation offered in
the belief of the continuity of life beyond our earthly
pilgrimage. The sense of sorrow which confronts us on
each occasion is deepened as we look upon the grieving
faces, the mournful mementoes, and the tearful eyes that
memorial services inevitably invoke. The comforting
feeling comes from the knowledge that our immortality
is guaranteed through the enduring value of: **Torah and
maasim tovim** and through the transmitting to posterity
the spiritual goals for which we strive.

The consciousness of immortality becomes multiplied
when applied on a large scale that includes a whole people's aspiration for survival. Judging by this standard
of deathlessness, our people can point to a remarkable
record of tenacity in which we have achieved the almost
impossible aim of maintaining, unbroken, the golden
chain of Jewish tradition under conditions and circumstances which would have torn apart other peoples.

In the life—cycle of other nations, the clinging to national existence is manifest in the endeavor to hold fast
to one's native soil, enlarging the same whenever possible.
Employing the philosophical concepts of Time and Space, ·
the land-hungry peoples of the earth have ever sought to
satisfy their yearnings in increasing search for Space.
In this spatial ambition, man has taken literally the injunction of Genesis: "And thou salt conquer the earth
and have dominion over it". Mortal man constructs the

means whereby he is able to descend into the abysmal depth of the sea, and builds artificial wings with which to span the sky—all for the express purpose of claiming ever greater portions of the earth's space. Within recent months, a rapidly re-arming Germany has reclaimed the Saar Territory, occupied the Sudenten land, absorbed the remnants of Austria, and now seeks to disrupt the peace of the earth by making insistent demands on Poland. This clamorous demand for more and more territory threatens the peace of humanity, as we do not know what incident or which provocation will touch off the spark that will once more plunge the world into darkness and mankind into sorrow.

The attitude of our own people presents a refreshing contrast, for throughout our national existence, we knew little of the yearnings for Space beyond the legitimate hopes for the conquest of the Homeland. Otherwise, in the philosophic sphere of Space, the desires of the Jew were always limited. A dramatic demonstration of this attitude is gleaned from the dictum of our sages regarding the conquests and exploits of King David. It was the lasting accomplishment of the poet, Prince of Israel, to liberate Jerusalem, and thus he set the stage for the culmination of a great dream:

"And I will build a house in the name of the Lord, the God of Israel".

In his patriotic zeal, King David went somewhat beyond the narrow boundaries of the Holy Land as described in the Bible, attaching to the territory of Eretz Israel a stretch from neighboring Syria. Instead of praising King David for this seemingly heroic adventure, the wise men of the Talmud question the validity of these conquests:[2]

---

2. Talmud Gittin 47b.

They doubted whether these conquests were of a binding nature and were, indeed, loath to invest these newly acquired territories with the characteristic attributes of the Holy Land. It is not strange that they should have done so, in spite of the veneration in which the son of Jesse was held. For they could point to King David's own words in the Scriptures in challenging the wisdom of territorial aggrandizement:

> "Unless the Lord build a house, in vain have its builders toiled therewith."[3]

What profiteth nations to conquer lands and to despoil territory, unless the enduring quality of their gains is vouched by more than human authority? What guarantee exists that the spectacular gains and bloody conquests of Nazi Germany will be any more permanent than the fruits of the Blood and Iron policy that crumbled into dust with the debacle of 1918?

The whole sweep of Jewish thought and ideology is foreign to expansionism in Space, and it has always placed the emphasis upon qualitative acquisition rather than upon quantitative gain. The very creation of our universe as envisaged by the authors of the Midrash contained the abiding lesson that it is the **kind** of world that counts, and not the **size** of the world. Commenting upon the symbolic significance of the divine name **Shaddai**,[4] they trace its origin to the desire upon the part of the world to expand beyond its present confines at the birth-hour of the cosmos when out of the void and vague space-lessness, the heavenly command brought forth the spheres and the realms which are part of the universe.

It is characteristic of the thought processes of the Jew

---

3. Psalms 127, 1.
4. Talmud Hagiga 12.

that the name, whose vernacular connotation is "Almighty" is associated not with limitless expansion, not with boundless growth, not with endless advancement, but with prescribed narrowed existence, as if to bring home the deathless refrain that not the large in extend, not the great in territory, and not the big in authority is necessarily the righteous, the just, and the admirable.

Our guide-post which served as the beacon light for our people in determining national policy with regard to survival and immortality is reflected in the words of the prophet Habakkuk whose peroration comprises this morning's Haphtarah: **Omad vaymoded oretz**[5]—"He stood and measured the earth." There is but so much to the earth and no more, and if man arrogates to himself more than his allotted share in Space:

"He saw it and drove nations asunder".[6]

Time and again have people aspired for world conquest, but their ravenous desires were not long satisfied. The strongest of empires, the mightiest of commonwealths have crumbled as we read further in the prophetic homily:

"The eternal mountains were shattered, and the hills had to bow."[7]

Nations that loomed large on the horizon of the world, countries which seemed as strong as the Rock of Gibralter were shattered by the Will of God, and those seemingly everlasting, like the hills, had to bow when God decreed that the end must come to man's grasping, groping, grabbing, and gnawing grip upon the limited territories of the world. For God Alone had eternal possession: **Ki li kol haaretz.**

---

5. Habakkuk, III, 6.
6. Ibid.
7. Ibid.

The Jew, who has ever regarded sceptically the spatial ambitions of his fellow humans, is fully aware of the limitations of the globe, and is never in the forefront when man ventures forth for conquest. It is in consideration of Time that the Jew feels ever at home, knowing that Time marches on, on his side. This was and is his greatest consolation and most assuaging comfort. When the present seemed bleak and dreary, he could always find promise and expectation in a world of tomorrow, in a time yet to be. The designers of the New York World Fair who captivated the imagination of America with their graphic exposition of the marvels and wonders that will characterize the world of the future, realized but little that the very title of this wonderful exposition is borrowed from the vocabulary of the Jewish Hopes.

The harassed and haunted Jew, whose humble but inspiring Palestine—Pavilion envisions his dreams of tomorrow, hopes against overwhelming odds that this "World of Tomorrow" will bring his millenium nearer. Furtively he asks, will it bring this new world? or will it be another step backward with more crushing blows, with more tragic disappointments, with more heart-breaking experiences? We do not know what the future holds in store for us, but we always view Jewish history in the perspective that suggests hopes predicated upon a world of tomorrow. The slave mothers in Egypt, the weary wanderers in the desert, those who sang their sublime song of sorrow by the waters of Babylon, the ones who perished by the sword of Rome, and the hundred generations that followed them from exile to exile, these had little enough comfort in their harrowed lives; they drew their solace by probing deeply into the recesses of the past, and found sustaining strength by peering into the vista of the future.

In its philosophical connotation "Tomorrow" implies

Time limits. And to the Jew, it speaks with the wisdom of Solomon "There is a time and season for everything". Someday there will come to the Jew a time of rejoicing and a season of liberation. In this world of strife and sorrow, we Jews, whose souls have suffered so much, must still pray and hope for a happier tomorrow, nay, we must make a way for it by exhibiting the torch of light in a world of dismal darkness, by evidencing high hopes in the face of defeat and despair, and by practicing gracious charity in a cruel and calculating age.

Thus shall be gathered, someday, the broken remnants of humanity and the scattered fragments of Israel, when the people of God will know that the time of their sorrows is ended and the season of their rejoicing approaches. We can hasten the advent of that day with the principles set forth above and indeed make way for tomorrow by giving vital meaning to the words of the prophet Isaiah:

"Make way, clean the path, remove the obstructions from the road of my people."[8]

We believe, in perfect faith, that there will be a palace of peace for the Jew, and a better, happier, and more glorious World of Tomorrow.

---

8. Isaiah LVII, 14.

FOOTPRINTS OF THE PAST

THE genius of the Jew, which has carried him across the seemingly impassable barriers of exile and homelessness, has also enabled him to bridge the chasm between this world and the next by viewing the latter as the spiritual continuity of an existence which was heretofore, both physical and spirit-like. This sense of sequence manifests itself more potently in the philosophy of Jewish existence by connecting every new generation with its forebears. This association effectively forges the golden chain which carries the stream of Jewish consciousness down through the corridor of the ages. This is, in essence, the content of the Yiskor service and innumerable are the credits recorded in the Ledger of our souls because of our communion with these great spirits of Eternity upon whom we lean today for moral uplift and a measure of inspiration. It is a healing tonic for our sorely distressed hearts to close our eyes for a few fleeting moments and relax in the soothing glow of motherly love and fatherly affection which once was ours, thus bringing to life once more the spiritual strength of our early years.

The Yiskor prayers would fail in their purpose if their total effect consisted only of bathing our weary souls in the refreshing waters of a sweet and tender yesteryear. To be true to its design, this solemn observance should help fashion the patterns of our present existence by making us lean more heavily upon our spiritual heritage. To achieve the full religious import of Yiskor, the service must enable us to drink deeply of ancient wisdom, and teach us to adjust into closer harmony the experiences

(98)

of our modern lives with those of the generations preceding us.

The sense of this Eternity has ever been the foundation stone of Jewish religious thought, and our Sages expressed it in terse and telling words when they speak thus in the Midrash: **Lomo nimshlu yisrael l'geffen**— "Why is Israel compared to a vine?"[1] they elucidate. "Just as the ripening grape must lean upon a dead vine to grow new fruit, so must Israel lean upon its past history".[2] In this simple though effective peroration of our Sages, they summed up the full meaning of our historic immortality. Israel learned upon its past when it accepted the Torah at the foot of the mountain. Solomon supported himself upon the memories of his distinguished forebears when he built a Holy Temple.[3] When our parents and grandparents recited Yiskor, they were leading the type of lives that harmonized with the lives of those in whose hallowed memory they chanted these sacred prayers. Look around in the Synagogue today and compare the people who want to connect their existence with the lives of those who lived before them in order to continue the unbroken march of forty centuries of Jewish life. What a disheartening picture, what a frightening occurrence. People come to say Yiskor, but in their lives the light of Israel's spirit has been all but extinguished. The incidents and texts quoted above dealt with a vibrant, pulsating, fully alive generation who resembled in every respect the previous generation. Thus there was a communion of kindred souls at every Memorial Service, as well as at every other occasion when the religious practices of their times brought them in spiritual harmony with their departed ones. What a sad spectacle we behold today. Those people who say

---

1. Midrash, Psalms 80, 9.
2. Ibid.
3. Talmud: Shabbos, 30a.

Yiskor today have within their number a great majority who differ completely from those they wish to honor. The Shabbos is a forgotten item in their lives. They have forgotten that those parents they mourn and reverence would not even be able to break bread with them, if by some miracle, they could come back from the grave. Too, too many of our young people and many of our old people have forgotten the traditions of our ancient nation. Our Jewish men have forgotten what a pair of tephillin are like, and our daughters of Israel are insensitive to the finest traditions of religious Jewish womanhood. It is a generation whose very soul has been deadened and whose spirit has become callous with the cynicism engendered by the bleak realities of the present. It is a devastating feeling to realize that those who have died a religious death lean so heavily upon those who have experienced a physical death but who are born again in their immortality. A vast segment of American Jewry is so completely cut off from the religious practices of our faith that to all intents and purposes, they are like a withered branch of a once blossoming tree. It is a strange spectacle indeed to see the spiritually dead resting upon the physically dead.

We may ask ourselves if there is only despair for us if we try to realize a better integrated Jewish life in this beloved land of ours or should we give up hope? Is there an avenue of escape and a road of hope which can be sought in order to bring back to protecting folds of our faith those who have strayed from it?

In the second book of Kings, we read of a most remarkable incident. It concerns a burial procession that was attacked by a band of desperadoes. The mourners cast the body of the person into the cave where the Prophet Elisha had been interned:

"And as the man came into contact with the bones of Elisha he revived and was upon his feet."[4]

Our Sages in the Talmud question the particular merit of this man and conclude that:

"He was fond in his lifetime of a quaint and important practice of kindness. He would fill his bags with drinking water, station himself at the crossroads, and offer each passerby a healthful and refreshing drink."[5]

My friends, the highways of the world today are crowded with our hounded and stricken co-religionists, who are not only in need of food and drink, but whose bodies have been mangled with a thousand reeling blows, their souls have been numbed and scarred, their hearts have been broken into the horrible pieces of stark tragedy that harassed their lives. American Jewry by its help, extended through its great humanitarian agencies that are strategically posted at all the crossroads of the world, is bringing healing to their woes. I have seen pictures of the pitiful orphans who arrived in Palestine exhausted from their flight through Teheran. As their trains passed through the cities of the Near East, soldiers of the United Nations gave them candy so as to sweeten in an infinitesimal measure their bitter portion. Such a soldier is a modern Shalom Ben Tikvoh who supplied the weary wanderers with refreshing drinks. We can become such givers of life, if we will contribute effectively and extensively to the United Jewish Appeal Drive now taking place in our city. Not only will our timely and speedy aid revive those who falter in their flight, but it will revive our sagging spirits, and we too, just like the man who came into contact with Elisha's

---

4. Kings 11, 13, 9.
5. Ibid., Yalkut Shimoni.

bones, will come to live and breathe again in the purified air of Jewish religious activeness.

Recently I read of a thrilling chapter in the magnificent history of this war, which abounds in stories of our brave and heroic soldiers. The story is told of a small detachment of American soldiers which was doing a special problem in the mountains of Colorado. In the group were several Jewish boys and as the Passover Festival was approaching, they asked for special provisions. Due to a severe snow-storm, it was found impossible to deliver the holiday foods to the group which was now stranded. But an Army Air Transport plane took off, located the soldiers, and dropped the Festival packages where the men could reach them. It is truly an inspiring experience to read the letters of thanks sent by these boys. They referred to these packages as veritable "manna from Heaven". Lest it be misunderstood, these boys were not suffering from physical hunger so that these packages meant so much to them. No! They were anxious for the matzos and other reminders of happier Pesachs because their souls demanded a satisfying remembrance. However, our brothers and sisters overseas, men and women such as you, are suffering from sheer physical hunger too. Their mental anguish is augmented by the knowledge that their helpless dear ones are dying under their feet from starvation. The little packages of food and drugs which are sent to them by the Joint Distribution Committee, the Vaad Hatzolah, and other agencies are the real "manna for Heaven". These packages sustain them and save their souls through the knowledge that they are not forsaken. In helping them to return to the land of the living, we become alive anew in the reflection that we have been instrumental in helping another human being to live. By remembering the injunctions of our Sages and proving ourselves true numan beings, we become akin to those righteous and charitable people of old. We are now in sacred spiritual contact with those whom we loved so much. Now is our chance to restore our spiritual health as we bring timely succor to those whose burden of life has become unbearable.

INVASION DAY SERMON

Preached at the Services of the United Orthodox Synagogues at
Congregation Sons of Abraham, June 6, 1944

A S WE turn our hearts to Him from Whom all blessings flow and Who is the Source of our salvation,
all of us have but one prayer, be it articulate or
silent, that He may safeguard the fighting sons of our
country and lead them to speedy and glorious victory.
Unto us, however, D-Day is THE DAY when we must
take into account our share in the unparalleled struggle
between the forces of righteousness and the powers of
evil; to us, this hour should speak in clear accents of
duty and responsibility of tasks and obligations.

In the weekly Portion of the Bible, we read the command of God unto Moses:

> "Make thee two trumpets of silver, of beaten work
> shalt thou make them that thou mayest use them
> for the calling of the congregation."[1]

The characteristic of these trumpets was that in their
physical makeup they were, in the Hebrew term
"Mikshah", hammered out of a single piece—i.e. fash-
ioned out of one bar, out of one solid piece of silver.
Two other ceremonial objects are spoken of in the Holy
Script which possess the same peculiar characteristic.
In the opening words of this week's reading, the laws of
the **Menorah** are delineated; "This was the work of the
Candelabrum—it was of beaten gold";[2] similarly, the
Cherubim over the Ark-cover, the angelic faces that
adorned the Holy Ark, were fashioned as a unity, and
not piece-meal.

---

1. Numbers X, 2.
2. Ibid., VIII, 4.

In these Biblical instructions we read the spirit of divine guidance that enables us to understand in full measure the true significance of the historic days in which we live. The first instruction of Scriptures speaks of the trumpet which sounded the clarion call to duty and which in our own day have summoned the millions of our sons and daughters who have answered the call. The summons to service must perforce be symbolized by an instrument which was formed out of a unified whole.

The lesson is imparted thereby that our country's defense can be safeguarded with success only when response to the trumpet call is in unison and when this is indeed "one nation indivisible", unitedly determined to hurl back the powers of darkness arrayed against us. We can state with a reasonable amount of certainty the deep-seated conviction that the men and women in the fighting forces are indeed united. They fight side by side regardless of creed, color, or geographic location.

Next, following the trend of our discussion, is the message of the Menorah, the sign of light and the harbinger of peace. The candelabrum, which America lights today and whose shining rays, we pray, will shed a warm glow over the face of the earth,—this light which is kindled as the sacrificial offering of our people to expel the darkness of mischief from the face of the earth—this light will shine in undisturbed glory when the hearts and souls of all Americans become united in a fervent prayer that the undoubted victory of our arms be followed by an enduring peace.

The last of the religious instruments that symbolize a unified ideal is the Cherubim. These angelic forms bore the facial expressions of young children, so say our

sages of the Talmud.[3]   It is no exaggeration to say that
the greatest single force in the attainment of the ideal
of unity is a consideration and a concern for the welfare
and happiness, for the future safety and security of our
children.   The heroic men who stepped ashore from the
landing boats this dawn, the men and women who crowd
the places of worship, and the architects and designers
of the future peace,—all are inspired with the hope and
imbued with the determination to make their world and
the world of the next generation—the world in which
our children and children's children will live—a better,
happier, and freer world.   The attainment of these
ideals requires that, in addition to the warriors who
fight, and in addition to their parents who pray, there
must also be the countless numbers of those who imagin-
ations are fired with the unity of purpose that underlies
the basic message of D-Day to us.   These patriotic
Americans must provide the sinews of war, the instruments of offense, and the implements of defense so essential for the successful continuance of the war effort.   It
is therefore both fitting and proper that we remind the
congregation of the forthcoming Fifth War Loan Drive,
which, in view of the tremendous needs, should be over-
subscribed, speedily and overwhelmingly.   And in conjunction with the law of lending to those in need, our
sages established a basic principle that although the
Hebrew word: "IM", normally implies a choice, in one
particular instance, it also indicates a compulsion.   When
Scripture instructs: "That if ye lend money to my
people",[4] that one particular "if" is a positive command,
rather than a voluntary choice.   This is especially true
now when the loans made to our country truly and all-
inclusively contain the element of: "my people", and its
success.   We are reminded as we are asked for the fifth
time for our help, that when the Israelites left the Egyp-

---

3. Talmud, Hagigah 13b.
4. Exodus, XXII, 24.

tian house of bondage, they too, were supplied with five sets of weapons: **B' chommesh minei klei zayan.**[5]

Now when Americans are about to assist the peoples of the world to break the chains of their slavery, the five essentials—the five weapons that we can provide are the five major loans promulgated by our country's leaders. Out of the amplitude of America's treasures and out of the magnitude of her heart will come the means of sustenance that will enable the enslaved nations of the earth to breathe the free air of God's beautiful world. Thus we shall not be looked upon as heretofore, as the Shylocks of mankind, but instead, a grateful and salvaged humanity will say: "The Gold of that land is indeed good."[6]

In the spirit of our Scriptures, D-Day to our embattled heroes means triumphat duty; to us, here in the Synagogue, it is a day of Dedication to the high ideals of Americanism and of Judaism which stem from the Menorah; and to thoughtful Americans everywhere, who are enthused with the unity of ideals and who are mindful of the tasks and problems confronting future Americans, this is indeed a day of deliverance from the depths of degradation, from the debris of desolation, and from the despair of disappointment in which most of mankind finds itself.

The sacred trumpets created out of one unified whole, calling men to duty, symbolize the desperately needed unity for which America must strive, labor, and give generously of itself. Thus will be achieved the United Nation, the kind of nation that our valiant warriors dream of coming home to. And we pray that it will be very soon.

---

5. Yalkut Exodus, XIII, 18.
6. Genesis 2, 12.

REVERENT, NOT JUBILANT

Preached on V-E Day at the Community Dinner of the
Jewish Welfare Fund, Atlanta, Ga.

W E MEET tonight in a reverent mood to re-conse-
crate our efforts so that the ideals, for which this
war was fought and won at least in Europe, should
not be lost sight of. Our mood is not one of jubilation,
not only because we still face the ordeal of war in the
East, but also because the termination of hostilities on
the continent, has left in its wake such a dreadful desolation and woeful tragedy as has never been experienced by
humanity before.

I find myself at this moment a thousand miles from
my home and my people, to be with you on a mission of
mercy which has become doubly urgent because of the
war's end in Europe. It was only last Shabbos that we
read in our Synagogues that portion of the Bible which
contains the awesome curses that would befall people
who walked not in the Ways of God. All of these and
more have so tragically been realized in our time, and
this week we are still in Bamidbor; our people are still
wandering in the desert, and untold thousands of them
rivet their anguished eyes upon these blessed shores,
begging, if you please, that we help erase the bitter and
bloody scars caused by the ravages of the world's most
hideous tyranny.

Our feelings and emotions are necessarily mixed; tears
of joy commingle with tears of sorrow. Those of us, like
myself, who have loved ones in the far eastern theatre
of war, are pointedly aware of the trying days yet to
come, but all of us realize that the end of actual warfare
in Europe will reveal the aching wounds, the serried

souls, the bleeding hearts, of millions of our fellow Jews who were left behind by Nazi Despotism.

There will be little cause for jubilation unless we summon every ounce of our creative energy to build on the ravaged ruins staring us in our faces and make good wherever possible the terrible neglect and horrible indifference displayed by the world at large toward the first and most harassed victims of the now infamous New Order in Europe. If our campaign will gain added impetus from the world-shaking event of this significant day, and in consequence thereof we will enlarge the scope of our relief and reconstruction activities, then, and only then, will we be enabled to rejoice, even in the limited sense of the word.

I alluded a moment ago to the fact that the current weekly reading of Scripture is the opening selection of the Book of Bamidbor. It is worthy of note that the very first law found within the pages of this holy book deals with a census of the Jewish people. Following a similar injunction to count the Jews of Europe and assume the responsibility of caring for them, the task imposed upon us is so enormously significant that generations hence we will be judged as having been confronted with an opportunity of overwhelmingly proportions. Should we fail, the judgment of history will condemn us as a people who lived in great times but failed to comprehend the meaning of its days. If on the other hand we rise to the full stature of greatness and confront the task that faces us with courage and devotion, then indeed will our children and our children's children revere our name and call us blessed.

The Rabbis of the Talmud described such a situation by speaking of people who in their day have seen the rainbow. As little children, we were taught a special benediction that we were to recite when this phenomenon made its appearance on the distant horizon. Well do I remember having called one day excitedly to my father that the rainbow was in the sky and that he should come outside and recite the benediction. He then explained to me that not all of our great men regard such an appearance as a happy omen; some indeed feel that the coming of the rainbow is a sign that our generation is wicked enough to be destroyed, and only the Divine promise to Noah never to unloose a world inundating flood again keeps us from being destroyed.

My friends, we who beheld with our own eyes the flood of fire, the avalanche of tears, the torrent of blood flowing in our time, must in fact feel the warning that burns itself into our very bones. **B'yomecho niraso hakeseth.**[1]

The rainbow that came in our day has colors that speak of the red blood of the martyrs, the green envy of the despoilers of humanity, the yellow cowardice of pseudo Democrats, to mention but a few mementoes of an unworthy generation whose rainbow heralds Divine anger and human failing.

II

There is yet another and compelling reason that creates the mood of reverence rather in the tone of jubilation on this momentous day. Bridging as I do the distance between New York, which was the home state of our late—lamented president and where I too live overlooking the Hudson which he loved and by whose banks he sleeps, and you here in Georgia, a place which he considered his second home and where he indeed

---

1. Talmud Katuvoth 77 Rashi.

closed his tired eyes, I cannot but feel a sharp tinge of defeat in the sweet taste of victory. Our illustrious president, in his announcement of V-E Day this morning, nostalgically remarked, "If only Franklin D. Roosevelt could have lived to see it." It is difficult to portray our own sense of bereavement and the bewilderment of the scared remnants of hounded humanity in Europe whose ardent champion he was and who in their moment of liberation shed many a bitter tear of regret that their liberator is no longer here.

It is of their tears and the tears of millions of Americans that I want to speak for a moment. We who leaned upon him for moral support, we who trusted him and found that our trust was not misplaced, never fully comprehended the tremendous burden carried by the man who could not stand up without the aid of physical support. No greater tribute, no higher glory, no deeper reverence, can ever be paid to any man than to remark that the passing of that one individual left a nation of one hundred thirty million people with a sense of loneliness and despair. Yes, my friends, most of us wept unashamedly, others turned away their faces to maintain some composure in the face of overpowering tragedy, but the newspapers reported that the Guard of Honor, composed of battle trained overseas veterans, had about them two shining things—one was their fixed bayonets, and the other their tears that rolled freely down their cheeks. Even those who had faced death unflinchingly on the bluffs and beaches of Cassino could not hold back a tear when their commander-in-chief was going home forever. Our rabbis in the Talmud have caught fully the import of such tears—tears shed, not because of a beloved kin who had departed, but simply because a man who was good and true and just departs from the living. **Hamored demoas al odom kosher.**[2]

---

2. Talmud Shabbos 105b.

"The tears that one sheds over the passing of a
righteous man are gathered up by the Lord and
placed in the House of His Treasures."

We, my friends, have our own concepts and descriptions
for the treasures we like to gather, but in the Treasure
Cup of a Merciful God, the most precious pearls are the
tears that mortal man sheds over his fellows who leave
behind a legacy of righteousness.

It is of his great spirit that I want to speak, and of
his indomitable will to conquer all obstacles, for these
must become our inspiration in order that we may continue to build where others may destroy. These sentiments gain added meaning if we recall the words of the
prayer that the late president composed a year ago on
D-Day: "And let our hearts be stout to wait out the
long travail, to bear the sorrows that may come." Yea,
my friends, even the sorrows of his own passing, and
once more of his prayer, "Help us, O Mighty God, to
re-dedicate ourselves in renewed faith in Thee in this
hour of great sacrifice." With this unyielding spirit, we
must resolve to move steadily forward so that when
generations yet unborn look back upon our sacrificial
devotions and find them praiseworthy, our deeds in the
scale of destiny will not be found wanting.

THE RABBI'S MOST COMPELLING TASK

Preached at Induction Services on January 3, 1943

IT IS with deep sense of reverence that I accept the responsibility to lead this worthy congregation in these trying times. My emotions are especially stirred by the inspired charge at the hands of my honored father in whose ways I hope to follow.

If I were to state in concise terms the most compelling task facing the Rabbi today, I would say that his most singular obligation is to sustain his people with hope and courage, to guide them in the path that will enable them to fix their vision on the far horizon where hopeful signs abide and trust in God resides.

I

Yesterday we read in our Synagogues the immortal story of God's revelation to Moses on Mount Horeb. When our great Law Giver was attracted by the phenomenon of the Burning Bush, he exclaimed: **Osuroh noh voere.**[1] The term employed seems strange on the surface for it one seeks to unravel the mystery of a strange occurrence, he would naturally step closed for investigation and research. Moses instead exclaimed that he would remove himself a bit to get a better view, thereby implying that there are realms beyond the normal judgment of man where the causes and reasons, the purposes and motives, may not be readily discernible, and very often situations are brought into play whose roots are not in the immediate present but in the distant past or in the unfathomable future. It was more than

(113)

appropriate for him to take this distant view when he readied himself to perceive this wondrous experience. He thereby laid down the immutable law that things around him and facts about him will not satisfactorily solve the cosmic riddle that confronted him, for in the Miracle of the Burning Bush was portrayed Israel's remarkable destiny, burning, yet indestructible, continuously aflame yet perennially enduring. The Rabbi, if true to his test, must impress this flock with the faith that the ways of God are unlike our ways, and that things which appear confusing and disturbing in the present will make themselves clear when viewed from a distant attitude.

> His Purposes will ripen fast
> Unfolding every hour
> The bud may have a bitter taste
> But sweet will be the flower.

People of primitive mentality must have tangible evidence of things in order to believe in them, just as small children can not grasp any abstract ideas unless conveyed by means of vivid pictures and colorful projects. As we grow older, however, we can understand ideas through the media of words, and those richly endowed with a mature imagination can conceive of both the natural and the supernatural. Blessed are those amongst us who are equipped with a heightened awareness in the domain of the spirit that enables them to understand the footprints of eternity during their pilgrimage here on earth.

II

Holy Writ records the tragedy of a generation, many members of whom lacked this intuitive awareness spoken

---

1. Exodus 3, 3.

of above, who in consequence grew frantic, when the physical manifestation of leadership momentarily absented itself from their midst. When Moses ascended the Mountain to await the Godly gift of the Tablets of Law, the people counted the days for his promised return. Our Sages interpret the expression **Vayar hoom ki boshesh moshe**[2]—"And the people saw that Moses delayed to come," to mean **Bo shesh**, that the sixth hour had come when according to their computations their master should have made his appearance. When, however, he delayed coming, the Dor Hamidbor sensed a religious catastrophe and turned frantically to a golden idol which could become the tangible expression of the Divine leadership they craved.

How strangely different was the ability of Joseph, and how remarkable the degree of his religious inspiration that enabled him to remain steadfast in his loyalty, unflagging in his devotion, and faithful to the principles implanted in his breast by his father, even when he suffered banishment and exile. Our rabbis instruct us that Joseph was enabled to overcome fierce temptation because in the moments of despairing danger he conjured up the vision of his saintly father, and this enabled him to summon a special fortitude in critical hours and emerge triumphant in his battle with evil temptation. **D'muth d' yuknno shel oviv nirith lo.**[3]

III

Much of this strength to overcome the obstacles that clog our path to Godliness eminates from the spirit and the soul. Lest we be weakened by the crushing blows suffered in recent times, we must continually and in-

---

2. Exodus 32, 1.
3. Talmud Sotah 37.

9

variably turn to the pages of our sacred literature where
we may find the sustaining strength to help us carry the
oppressing burdens.   One of our spiritual heroes whose
words kept aflame the hope in our hearts was the prophet Isaiah who speaks in the sixth chapter of his book
of a new vision of God.   He too lived in trying days for
the words with which he introduces his peroration are
as follows: "It was in the year of the death of King
Uzziah"[4]   Now the death of a good king always presages
a change and very often a catastrophic one.   In those
turbulent days of royal departure, the ordinary mortal
would have caught gloomy connotations in the dismay-
ing turn of events.   The prophet rose to the highest
pinnacle of spiritual exaltation, and in the stirring
words of a flamboyant spirit, he exclaimed: "And I have
seen the Lord enthroned on a high and mighty throne."[5]
Little wonder then that the mystic students of sacred
Kaballah invested this peroration with the enthralling
symbols of their inspired philosophy and read into the
words of this vision the basic principles and the fundamental verities of our ancient and hallowed faith.   The
rabbi of today faces no greater task and can accomplish
no holier ennoblement than when in times of crises and
desperation, he can lead his congregants to the high
places so that they too can have a new Vision of God
and a new perception of His Holiness.

IV

In accepting your call and in dedicating myself to the
task ahead of us, I am aware that the ordinary limitations imposed upon the American rabbi have become
increasingly burdensome due to the increased tensions
caused by wartime conditions.   With so many of our

4. Isaiah 6, 1.
5. Ibid.

young ones in the armed forces, it devolves upon us at home to extend our finest energies for the maintenance and care, for the furtherance and cultivation, of those ideals for which they have gone forth to battle.

A singularly effective and timely quotation from the Book of Nehemiah will fully illustrate the all inclusive plea that I am making:

> "Those that built on the wall, and those that bore burdens, with those that loaded,—every one with one of his hands wrought on the work and with the other hand held a weapon."[6]

One hand of our people is forging the instruments of war to insure the supremacy of the ideals which actuated the founders of our country, the second hand must continue to build the sanctuary to God's Glory which will insure the spiritual stability and moral climate especially needed in these trying days. In these sacred endeavors I will need the help of every one of you. Man, woman and child can find a necessary spot in which to cooperate in these important activities.

There is an ancient legend that at the time of the rebuilding of the second temple to which our previous quotation alludes, there was a very old member of the tribe of the Levis who was unable to contribute his share of physical labor to the sanctified work because of his advanced old age, but he was anxious to share, and so, recalling the glorious days of the First Temple, he inspired the builders by singing unto them the selections with which the services in the sanctuary were accompanied in days gone by. Similarly, my friends, in our own hallowed activities, everyone's place is important and everyone's contribution will be significant. I be-

---

6. Nehemiah 4, 11.

speak the active cooperation of the men and women
whose activity guarantees the Synagogues' progress. I
plead for the entry of our young ones into these holy
portals, so that the innocent utterances of their un-
spoiled lips may resound in the House of God and
sweeten the try days which are ahead. I reverently
call for the prayers and the wisdom which come from
the tongues of our old and respected members who
remember the glory of the Jewish Synagogue and the
Holiness of the House of Learning in distant lands where
Judaism was based upon the wholesome, constant, and
complete devotion given it. Above all, I pray, that the
Graciousness of the Lord God may be upon us, may He
also establish upon us the work of our hands. Yea, the
work of our hands, may He establish it.   Amen

PRAYER DAY SERMON

Preached on May 13th, 1945, at the Union Services of the
Albany Orthodox Synagogues, Albany, N. Y.

A T THE request of our illustrious president and
commander-in-chief, Harry S. Truman, we have set
aside this hour for prayerful meditation and humble
gratitude to the Lord of Hosts by Whose Grace we were
able to complete at least one part of this terrible conflict. We are grateful, not because we are victorious in
ourselves, but because the ideals and principles for
which we have fought have emerged victoriously. We
are sublimely happy in the thought that in this horrible
carnage we are on the side of justice and humanity, and
not on the side of aggrandizement and self-seeking.

In this hour, America pauses, not only to pray for the
blessing of peace, but also to honor the mothers of our
country. This day is usually set aside in tender solicitude and poignant reverence to remind us of our gratitude to those faithful, heroic, and devoted women who so
loyally nurtured and guided us, and from whose loving
and understanding hearts we first learned how to pray.
Prayer-day exercises cannot be held on a more appropriate day than Mothers' Day. No segment of humanity
is more vitally concerned or more seriously and directly
effected by the tragic stream of contemporary happenings than our Mothers. These brave women,
whose hearts silently carry the scars and pain of
enforced separation from their children and the soul-
searing anguish of desperate waiting for word from
them, must sometime face the blinding shock which
shadows all of their remaining days, realizing that they
themselves have died a little notwithstanding their continuance of the now meaningless manifestations of life.

(119)

It is to these women, whose hearts were crushed when the evil tidings brought the tragic denoument which is part of war to their homes and who must travel the dark and silent night of sorrow and mourning, that I address my words. It is to these mothers whose throats whisper the sweet precious names of childhood memories despite the clogging choking dust whipped up by the furious storm of fire and smoke that is war, that I look to as I speak. It is of these human beings whose courage must equal that of the greatest hero and who must face the world and continue living though joy of life has left them at the graves of their beloved dead, that the Prophet speaks: "Mother upon sons was broken."[1]

To these mothers and to the mothers of generations still unborn do we owe the responsibility of achieving peace—a lasting, thorough, final peace. We must seek our way toward this objective with the same staunch determination and dogged loyalty with which our boys fight their gruelling battles. We owe our solemn obligations and our unceasing efforts to these mothers and to the sons who will never again return to the arms of their loved ones. Our failing energies must not flag; we must strengthen our hearts to determine that we will exert every ounce of our collective will to the goal of wiping out for all time the malignant cancer of facist ideology without any conciliatory compromise. It is up to us, the present generation, to sincerely resolve in the spirit of our prayers today, that we will not rest until the secure foundations of a just and world-wide security and peace is assured. The peoples of this old planet of ours have traversed a tortuous path between the machinations of evil and the fumblings of the ignorant. We must now all join in prayer that the Almighty Lord will help us to see the way and to understand the truth, thus giving us strength to follow the just way.

---

1. Hosea 10, 14.

My prayers are lesser than three
Nothing, I pray, but two
Give me O Lord eyes to see
Give me the Power to follow it through.

Just thirty days ago, the world lost a great leader and
a true man of the people. Today marks the completion
of the Sholoshim, the end of the thirty days period of
mourning for our fallen commander, Franklin Delano
Roosevelt. We miss him and we mourn for him as if he
were our own blood and flesh, but we are humbly grateful
that God in His Infinite Wisdom gave us the privilege of
living in his generation and learning from him the
essence and meaning of the concepts of humanitarianism
and true democracy. Again we must thank our Creator
that when our Captain was called to his Eternal Rest we
were so fortunate as to have a man of the calibre of
Harry S. Truman at our helm. Though we can understand and fully realize the truth of his words when he
said upon hearing the mournful tidings,

> "The weight of the Moon and all the Stars has just
> fallen on me."

thank God, under his guiding hand the crisis which our
Democracy faced in the crucial hour of President Roosevelt's passing has been met with historic equanimity.
President Truman has taken the reins in the orderly
Democratic process, thereby proving to the world that
the foundations upon which our Democracy rests are of
tested and proven strength. No matter the magnitude
of the crisis which might face our Democratic institutions, truly we can say, as was said at the time of the
completion of the thirty day period of mourning for our
leader Moses:

"And children of Israel wept for Moses in the plains of Moab for thirty days."[2]

The verse immediately following advises us: **V'yehoshua bin nun mole ruach chochmo**—"The spirit of Joshua has ripened into wisdom"[3] and our Rabbis in Midrash emphasize that it was due to the continued and beneficial influence by which the elder Prophet inspired his disciples and successors.[4] We are filled with a sense of security and safety in the knowledge that the present occupant of the White House will surely follow in the paths of his great predecessor and truly make his residence the Lighthouse of Human Hopes, whose reassuring beacons will penetrate the dark places of human fear.

Another mighty leader of ages past also dreamed of completing his glorious career by erecting a Temple to God which was to be dedicated to the love of humanity and to the ideals of peace. However it appears on the surface that those whose strength is sapped and whose powers are exhausted by the effort of achieving their great ideals in life cannot live to be the architects of the permanent structures of their hopes. So it is once more destined that a Solomon[5] of our times should continue to weave the sacred strands which go into the accomplishments of the dream of David. It is of David that Jewish tradition states that when his successor finally achieved his dream, and made himself ready to enter the portals of the hallowed precincts, he was unable to proceed as the gates would not open.[6] Not until the spirit of David, his predecessor, was conjured up by quoting his words and recalling his ideals would the doors of the sanctuary open. Similarly, if the plans currently made

2. Deuteronomy, 34:8.
3. Ibid., 9.
4. Idem., Midrash Rabba.

and the projects proposed should have permanence, they will have to be made in the spirit of the man who gave his life for the attainment of these ideals.

It is for us to hope, trust, and pray, that when the design will be drawn and the blue-prints proposed for enduring peace, the name of Franklin Delano Roosevelt will be invoked so that his sacrifice on the altar of humanity shall not have been in vain. This is the prayer of mankind in the solemn hour of Victory and Thanksgiving.

---

5. The President indeed, prayed with the words of Solomon in his first public address.
6. Talmud, Sabbath 31a.

VICTORY IN THE SPIRIT OF 1776

Sermon delivered at the Prayer for Victory Services and
Broadcast over Station WABY, July 4, 1943 at Albany, N. Y.

SOMEDAY a competent historian will write the
spiritual history of these United States. To do justice to his task he will have to read widely, ponder
deeply and unceasingly sift the factual data for the
discovery of spiritual patterns that are woven into
the matrix of our people's soul. My talk today concerns
itself with the one specific factor that makes itself apparent behind the story of the stirring events that
brought forth the cause of these patriotic exercises.

Even the briefest excursions into the field of colonial
history will reveal the startling fact that the dominant
figures in the drama of American revolutionary activities
were men who had little to gain in a personal sense,
from the establishment of an independent nation.
Several of the leaders were holding positions of honor,
others were men of great wealth who had everything to
lose in times of upheaval and during a period of inter-
nicine warfare. They were moved more by the plight
of their fellow men than by selfish motives, the burdens
laid upon their communities concerned them more than
their position or interest.

This attribute of selflessness is a primary prerequisite
for leadership in many environment tinged with idealistic connotations, and much of the world's pain and sorrow is caused by its absence from the council tables of
nations. Scriptural instruction ever a potent force in
the moulding of fine human characters has long since
established the norm which should become part of man's

(124)

spiritual baggage when anxious for ennoblement and inspiring leadership.

In the weekly portion currently read in our Synagogues we are introduced to the widely ramified ritual of the Red Heifer. Commenting upon the Scriptural terminology: **Zoth hatorah odom ki yomuth boahel**[1]—"And this is the Torah, if a man dieth in a tent." A reknowned Talmudic authority infers: **Omar resh lakish ain divri torah mithkaymin elo mimi shemeith atzmo oleho.**[2]

The Torah will have no guarantee for permanent survival only through the willingness of its proponents to sacrifice themselves for its sake. Thus was established the timeless truth that no set of ideals and no code of morals can long survive unless people place their maintenance and protection ahead of any personal motive of selfish considerations. No nation would have a chance for historical development unless and until profoundly inspired patriots place country above selfish desire, national welfare before individual comfort and communal good ahead of personal aggrandizement.

The heroic army of Washington encamped at Valley Forge, the brave men of Andrew Jackson who made the day of January 14th immortal behind the cotton fields of New Orleans, those who sleep at Gettysburg as well as the countless heroes of our own time who are imbued with the conviction that their sacrifices will help abolish the rule of despotism, our own boys and girls who only yesterday worshipped within these very portals, all placed the welfare of the social order ahead of their own personal comforts and desires. They give living reality and translate into daily experience the injunction of

---

1. Numbers 19, 14.
2. Talmud Brochoth 43b.

Resh Lakish, by removing self interest to ascertain and guarantee the enthronement of ethical and spiritual ideas. Though ours is commonly considered a callous and cynical age, there are still amongst us, countless men and women whose imagination is stirred by the highest consideration of human need and who, if made to choose, would prefer self sacrifice to the supposed security blandished by a slave civilization. One needs to think of our fearless pioneers in Palestine, the unsung heroes of the French underground, the reckless riders of the Russian guerilla army, the allied soldiers who voluntered to go ashore on the blood soaked beaches of Dieppe, as the reincarnated martyrs of saintly souls who since ages past have written large the epic of their days upon the sands of history and the footprints of time.

II

A most moving illustration of this attitude that places communal consideration above and beyond the personal motives of self seeking individuals is found in the Talmudic allegory where our Sages instruct us: **Meladed shekodash boroch hu nithatef seth atzmo k' shliach tzibur**—"That the Almighty Blessed be He, wraps Himself in the sacred vestments of an officiating Minister and speaketh to His children. If you will worship before Me in such a manner, I will surely come and forgive you your sins."[3]

Surely our Sages meant to convey a profound moral lesson when they implied that the Holy One, Blessed be He, Presents Himself in the habiliments of a Schliach Tzibur—but when we examine closely the historical evolution of the role that functionary plays in Jewish Religion Ritual and the significance attached to the prayers we

---

3. Talmud, Rosh Hashono; 17b.

chant, we quickly realize that it is not alone musical
erudition, nor tonal qualities that mark the venerated
qualification of the minister who leads the congregation in prayer. In the pristine beauty of his calling the
prime considerations are the ability and aptitude he pos-
sesses to pour for the fervent plea and heartfelt supplication of his people. Not as an individual does he implore
his Maker, he indeed officiates as the designated emissary of the worshippers called upon to express their un-
spoken thoughts and throbbing sentiments. The whole
wide range of Jewish liturgy in general and the hallowed
Chant of the Schliach Tzibur in particular is bereft of
individual motives, no substantial part hereof is tuned
to any one specific private personal plea. The whole
fabric of our prayer book is pitched on the far loftier
plane of everyone's needs and expressing as it be, the
vast expanse of human hopes, the broad field of human
desires, the limitless scope of human aspirations and the
ever recurrent faith that the Lord be Enthroned above
all His Creation and the lot of all mankind and not that
of any one particular group of special individual be improved. If God appears unto us in the guise of a
Schliach Tzibur, it is merely for the urgency of in-
structing us to pray, to plead, to hope and to dream not
alone for ourselves but for our fellow men as well, indeed
for them first and for us thereafter. Our Sainted
Teachers conjure up this soul stirring allegory, blazing
the trail towards deeper devotions by the abiding moral
lesson that when we address ourselves to the Heavenly
Throne of the Ruler of the Universe for pity and compassion or in expressions of human longing, emphasis
should be placed and ascendancy granted not for the individual plea but for common need.

Similarly the signers of the Declaration of Independence whose anniversary we observe today, pledged their
lives, fortunes and sacred honor, thus they established

the conviction that in consonance with the Scriptural inspiration and Talmudic idealisms developed above, they too, were ready and prepared to sacrifice all that life held dear, so that the spirit of human progress would advance in their times. They, too, in their day, prayed for victory but in the wake of that victory they craved to introduce an unprecedented experience in human relationship. They sought to, eradicate the bigotries and prejudices of the old world and to weave into the texture of the new American Civilization, the fine strands of political democracy and equality of opportunity denied to so many in the old world.

We who are privileged to be their spiritual descendants and the rightful heirs of their idealism should pray with assurance strong, not only for the speedy conclusion and victorious termination of strife on foreign battle fields but for the continuance and the further development of the ideals of a free society here at home where we are called upon not only to supply sinews of war but to give zealously the last remaining ramparts of freedom in a battle scarred world.

We too, must dedicate our all as did the Founding Fathers on that historic July 4th, to the proposition that all men are created equal. Victory in the spirit of '76 must mean the end of this bloody war by preaching a false doctrine and by spreading a dangerous theory of government. Victory in the Spirit of 1776 will mean a reevaluation of the selfless idealism that motivated the men of that age whose vision and victory made these blessed shores the haven of the oppressed and the refuge of the persecuted.

Let us pray that in God's good time and with the hastened return of our loved ones we shall not only be triumphant on land, on sea and in the air but we shall again turn our welcome hand to the down trodden of the earth as we said in the years gone by,

> Give me your tired, your poor, your huddled masses, yearning to be free, the wretched refuse of your teeming shore. Send these homeless tempest tossed to me. I lit my lamp beside the golden door.[4]

4. Emma Lazarus.

WINGS OF DAWN

Sermon delivered for the Officers' Candidates at
the Army Air Force Technical Training Command,
Miami Beach, Florida, June 28, 1942

IT IS always the mark of spiritually strong men and women that they can face adversity with courage akin to simple bravery. These are the people who know how to redeem bad times and provide themselves with shields against despair on occasions when sorrow looms menacingly over the horizon. In the difficulties and tribulations that America experiences today, the frail in hope see the dying sun, whereas those who face unflinchingly the world, see in the struggle between light and darkness the awakening dawn, upon whose wings are ushered in Hope and Trust.

A similar spiritual fortitude helped Moses of old to confront the evil doers of his day and to face with equanimity those who plotted the destruction of righteousness and the enthronement of evil. Rising to majestic splendor, in the supremacy of his faith, he spoke to rebellious Korach and his followers: **"Boker v'yoda ashem es asher—Lo"**—"In the morning, the Lord will make known who belongs to him."[1]   Temporary set-backs and momentary defeats did not dismay the trusted servant of God, and his soothing words speak to us this very day, inspiring us to await confidently the coming of the morning "Boker" which will see the warming rays of the sun, dispel clouds of gloom, and the strength of light displace the abysmal forces of darkness. It was ever so in Israel's history and our people learned to look for the morrow when Today seemed stained with despair.

---

1. Numbers XVI, 5.

To the enslaved multitudes in Egypt, Moshe Rabenu
brought the tidings of impending redemption when he
assured them "Mochor Yihyeh Hoos Hazeh". The sign
of God's deliverance will be evident tomorrow and the
mark of our people's redemption will be clearly visible
when the sun of liberation will shine anew upon humanity now in chains.

We alluded a moment ago to the incident in the life
of Moses when his leadership was challenged, his authority questioned, and his spiritual sovereignty threatened. There may have been many in the entourage of
the law-giver who trembled upon seeing the imposing
array of personalities who joined hands to uproot the
established order of Israel's existence. They were indeed in the words of Scripture "Princes of the Congregation, the elect men of the Assembly and men of renown."[2]
Indeed, possessed of Universal renown, as the Talmud
states: **Shehoyoh lohem shem b'chol haolam.**[3] Similarly
today, men of many countries, strong and powerful nations, countries which enjoyed considerable renown
among the civilized brotherhood of humanity such as
Italy, the home of the Rennaissance, Germany, the path-
finder in many sciences, Japan, which seemingly com-
bined the civilization of both east and west, these, together with their satellites, apparently set out to challenge, as Korach did, the supremacy of law and order, of
truth and decency in human affairs. We would be untrue to the memory of the hallowed martyrs of our people and to the warriors of freedom in every land if we
should falter in the face of the challenge flung at us; we
should rather armor ourselves with the promise proclaimed by Moses and spoken by God, "And it shall come
to pass that the man whom I have chosen, his rod will
blossom". We who fight on the side of justice pray that

2. Ibid. 2.
3. Talmud Sanhedrin CXa.

the choice of God may dwell upon us, and that through the grace of His abundant blessings, our cause shall prosper and our efforts prevail.

THE BIBLICAL IDEAL OF LEADERSHIP

Preached at The Officers' Candidates' School at
Miami Beach, Fla., July 5, 1942

L AST week we discussed the Biblical ideal of association and cooperation between the nations of the
earth, as well as their mutual responsibility to one
another. Today, I would like to continue the same
thought and point to an incident in this week's portion
of the Law which delineates in broad strokes, the ideals
of leadership characteristic of Moses. These are especially essential today when you, gentlemen, are preparing yourselves for leadership in the crucial times ahead.

The one single factor and the leading attribute that
characterizes the leadership of Moses throughout his
long and distinguished career was that of selflessness or
self abnegation. Everything for the people and nothing for himself. He was consumed with a burning desire and an ardent anxiety to serve those entrusted to
his care, regardless of the toil or tribulation, the trials
or self-denials that it would entail. We read, indeed,
how Moses asked the Lord to appoint a successor to him:

"May the Lord, God of all the spirits, appoint a man
over the Congregation."[1]

"So that the Congregation of the Lord may not be like a
flock without a shepherd". A lesser man than Moses
might have brooded over his inability to enter the Holy
Land. A Man of smaller stature might have sulked at
being denied the privilege of seeing the Promised Land
—but not Moses. His only concern was the happiness
and the safety of the people over whose destinies he pre-

---

1. Numbers XXVII, 16.

sided for decades. Not the satisfaction of his own desires was paramount in his concern; he did not busy himself nursing the wound in his soul and the disappointment in his heart. Instead, he set our resolutely to
complete the task as far as he could and to make sure
that the fate of the people of God would continue to be
in trustworthy hands.

The Rabbis of the Midrash envision this unselfish
spirit of our great master and interpret the very blessings which he bespoke before taking leave from his
earthly associates. Commenting upon the scriptural
term **V'zos habrocho**—"And this is the blessing"[2] they
ask "Who was meant by King David when he stated:
"He shall carry the blessing from the Lord".[3] In the
case of Moses, they tell us that we ought not to read
Yiso but instead **Yasi** caring for others, always caring
for his fellowmen, ever anxious to look for their needs,
totally oblivious to his own personal desires, and im-
mersed completely in the troubles and anxieties of the
people under his command. Such, indeed were the
ideals of leadership that were symbolic of the whole
existence and the entire career of our great Law-giver.
They are the self-same standards of leadership for which
the world cries out today and the sincere application of
which can alone bring to our troubled world a full
measure of healing and salvation.

Sometimes, I like to carry a little further the dream
of Moses and its subsequent realization by his trusted
Lieutenant Joshua—who was to succeed him and successfully lead the Israelites into the land of their fathers.
It was only a generation ago that our fathers were inspired by the breath-taking idealism of President Wilson
who hoped to lead all mankind into a better pasture. He,

2. Deuteronomy XXXIII, 1.
3. Psalms XXIV, 5.

like Moses was not permitted to carry into reality the high resolves of his inspired vision, but he, like Moses, had a trusted lieutenant, who, by resistless determination was able to translate into factual existence the inspiration of the Master. Our commander-in-chief today, served under President Wilson. From his early youth he was saturated with Wilsonian idealism. May he be privileged, as was Joshua, to give meaning to the masterful plan of his great mentor. May he be the Joshua of our age, and may the spirit of God rest upon his handiwork, so that he can lead us and the world into the promised land of our hopes.

WE ARE NOT ALONE

Preached at the Services of the Officers' Candidates' School at
Miami Beach, Sunday, July 12, 1942, by
RABBI ABRAHAM A. KELLNER

O NE OF the remarkable consequences of this global
war, in which all of us in one sense or another are
engaged, has been the reduction in distances and
the bringing closer to our doors of events that take place
ten thousand miles away. If any beneficial results
accrue from this catastrophic holocaust, it will be that
mankind will be brought closer together, and that people
who, in physical distance, may be far from us but whose
problems and perplexities are akin to ours, will be regarded as our next door neighbors. Thus the heroic
people of China are found to have numerous things in
common with us; and though, ideologically, we may be
far apart from the Soviet theory of State, nevertheless
we have joined hands with the Soviets to eliminate
Fascist aggression from the face of the earth. When
air-craft carriers can stealthily cross a three-thousand
mile gap of water to send their winged destruction to
peaceful lands, it is foolhardy to talk of isolation, and
futile to consider the oceans as effective protective barriers against barbaric onslaught.

Our world which suffered so much has indeed been
blighted by the ailment whose symptoms are primarily
manifest in setting apart race from race, peoples from
peoples, and nations from nations. There were times
when certain countries glorified in splendid isolation.
Now we are rapidly approaching the dream when mankind's watchword will be "Splendid Cooperation". It
was only yesterday that we read in the Biblical portion
of the week of an incident in Israel's checkered history

(136)

whose reverberations still echo in the tortured ears of
humanity today.   We are told of King Balak who im-
ported the soothsayer Baalaam to put a curse on Israel
and thus remove their ability to withstand an attack.
This hired hand of a wicked king spoke in parables and
in ambiguous oracles.   All of his curses were dressed in
the clothing of admiration.   Thus he said to Israel:
"Behold a people dwelleth alone, and among the nations
it is not counted".[1]   This concealed condemnation may
have been worded to present Israel in the garb of
strength and independence, intimating that it had no
need of the association of other peoples and the cooperation of other nations.   In reality, however, this too was
meant as a slur on the escutcheon of Israel rather than
a compliment.   Furthermore, it was manifestly untrue,
since the whole wide scope of the laws of the Hebrews is
all-inclusive in nature and unifying in spirit.   Thus we
are enjoined to love the stranger and to protect the
poor and to support the needy of every faith and creed.
When King Solomon built the Temple, he instituted
offerings and sacrifices for all nations of the earth, and
did not choose to make that hallowed place a chauvinistic
hunting ground for self adoration.   The Talmud goes
even further and considers it a serious crime to stand by
when others are in trouble.   We are told that Pharoah,
before promulgating the cruel decree of drowning every
newly born Hebrew boy, consulted with his advisors.
When Baalaam advised this horrible step, Job stood by
and kept silent.   He did not openly acquiesce, perhaps,
with this dastardly act, but he was apparently too weak
to raise the voice of protest.

"And because he was silent at such a critical moment
such a severe punishment was visited upon him."[2]

---

1. Numbers XXIII, 9.
2. Talmud Sotoh 13.

It is perhaps not too far-fetched to assume that the pangs and pains of the world today have come upon us because the mighty nations of the world stood silently by when the maddened Fuehrers of Fascism uprooted whole peoples and vented their insane fury upon the defenseless minorities.

Mine is the hope and ours is the fervent prayer that out of this crucible of pain and sorrow which the world experiences today, there will shine forth a deeper consciousness of the responsibility that we owe to our fellow men. Thus will our sacrifices not be offered in vain if we will learn the abiding lesson that the peoples of the world, alone, live in a vale of tears, but together and united, they dwell in sunlit spaces of Hope.

THE LONG ROAD TO GLORY

Preached at Services For Enlisted Men of the Army Air
Forces at Beth Jacob Congregation, Miami Beach, Fla.
on July 19, 1942

THOSE familiar with the Jewish Calendar are aware
that, from the Jewish religious point of view, the
week which precedes the ninth day of Ab is marked
with sad mementoes and sorrowful moments. The
solemnity of the observance is eased only by the thought
and made bearable only by the knowledge that at the
end of the long hard road through which Israel's destiny
leads our people, there awaits us the glory of victory
and the comforting solace that is contained in the words
of the prophet: **Nachamu, nachamu ami**—"Comfort Ye,
Comfort Ye my people."[1]

You members of the American Army are in a sense
inspired by a similar hope. The road before us will
not be easy; the path is fraught with danger and diffi-
culty; but as sure as the sun shines, we are convinced
that ultimately, the effort and offering of the American
people will bear ample reward in the triumphant finale
which will certainly cap our endeavors.

Some people indeed prefer the easy way and the short
cut with the immediate results of gain and conquest.
Such, no doubt, is the motivating force of our enemies
both in the East and in the West, who have conquered
great stretches of territory and subjugated millions of
people. They have foolishly believed that Fate would
permit them not only to enjoy the fruits of their conquests but also to spread even further the poisoned
tentacles of their grasping reach. The rabbis in the

---

1. Isaiah 40, 1.

Midrash, in commenting upon Jeremiah's lamentations which will be intoned in the Synagogues a week from today, tell the story of a young wanderer, who, coming to a cross-road inquired of an old man standing by which road he should follow; the wise man responded: "This one is short but long; the other road is long but short."[2] The democratic peoples of the earth, by choice and necessity, have selected the long road which contains many obstacles and presents seemingly insurmountable hindrances, but in the last and final analysis, it will be the shortest road for it leads to just goals, righteous aims, and sanctified purposes. In reality, every person's life is possessed of a similar choice. Man is born and aims for achievements worthy of his finest endeavors. Between the two focal points of one's existence, namely birth and death, many lines can be chosen. We learn in the elementary lessons of geometry that the shortest distance between any two given points is a straight line. The straight life, the right life between the moment of our birth and the termination of our earthly pilgrimage is the most direct line. But this road, too, may at times be long in that it requires long suffering, patient endurance, persevering efforts, renstless and determination. Conversely, we find many a short road which in the last count became long, arduous, and tortuous, because the straight line was not the objective. Such was the experience of our forefathers in their wandering through the Arabian desert. In the Biblical Portion assigned for this week, Moses recounts their journeys, and comments upon their wanderings. At one time he tells us, an eleven day journey was completed in only three;[2] that was when the people were enthused with sacred inspiration to receive the Law of God, and to acquaint themselves with its precepts. When they turned from the straight road, however, and grumblingly chose to follow

2. Deuteronomy 1, 2; Roshi

their own hearts' desires, a seemingly short distance took forty years to traverse.[3]

We need to repeat and to restate these ancient verities. It is good for us to familiarize ourselves with the life-story of our ancestors so that in our own daily contact with the problems that confront us, we should be encouraged and inspired, and enthused with the knowledge, realization, and conviction that although the prospects may be for a long and dreary war, though the road that we must traverse may be complicated and tortuous, and though the difficulties that we must overcome may be numerous and exasperating, in the end, there awaits us, glory and victory, happiness and exaltation, and the assurance of the Scriptures: "Ye shall not fear them for the Lord your God He is the One who will battle for you." [4]

---

3. Psalm 95, 10.
4. Deuteronomy 3, 22.

WAR'S PURPOSE

Delivered at Friday Night Services, Dow Field,
Army Air Base, July 17, 1943

A PECULIAR sideline of war-time religion is the comment often made by cynical observers, namely, that since both sides in a great battle implore the blessings of God, the answer to both cannot possibly be made. President Lincoln was aware of this anomaly and referred to it in moving terms in his classic Second Inaugural Address. We who are engaged in this frightful war are convinced that our cause is just and that our goal is honorable. As we worship here in this Chapel tonight, we do not set ourselves up as the judges of our respective causes; instead, we turn to the prophetic reading of this Sabbath, and use the immortal words of Micah as the yard-stick with which to measure the degree of righteousness which accompanies our arms:

> "It had been told to thee, O Man, what is good, and what the Lord doth require of thee, only to do justice and to love mercy and to walk humbly with thy God."[1]

The enemies of our nation who are locked in mortal combat with all the Democratic peoples of the earth certainly do not measure up to the prophet's description. They have perpetrated unspeakable injustices against defenseless minorities; mercy, even only as a word, is non-existent in their vocabularies, and the arrogance with which they seek to impose their will upon all mankind is the direct antithesis of the standards set forth as the prerequisite of Goodness.

---

1. Mica, 6, 8.

Our case is not proven, however, merely by establishing the culpability of our adversaries. We must, ourselves, at all times remember to strive for the ultimate goal which is peace for all mankind. The first prayer in tonight's Service is the traditional Sholem Aleichem chant which is a welcome-song to the angels of Peace who are ever hovering above us, even in these days of total war.

You men of the Air Force, who have dominion over the skies, have proved your peaceful intentions by preparing for peace, praying as King David prayed, "Who can endow me with the wings of the Dove, that I may fly and Rest."[2] Because of compulsion and not through any choice of our own, we are developing the world's mightiest airforce, whose avowed aim it is to clear the Heavens of the birds of prey who seek to enslave the entire globe. Now and for the duration, you must pray that you be endowed with the swiftness of the eagle to carry out your exacting task. Your flights and your missions are not the ultimate end, however. The closing words of the Psalmist allude to rest, to peace, and to the achievement of its goals, for which America girds her loins. As I address you, I think of you, not merely as masters of airplanes and experts in the art of warfare, but as the harbingers of a better day, whose actions will translate our ideals from the fabric of dreams into the texture of reality. Inspired with such Zeal, we can regard the battle-scarred deck of a ship, the breach of a firing gun, and the throttle of a bombing plane, as instruments of which the immediate purpose is destruction, but which will eventually become the very implements of construction, and will help us lay the foundation for a better world. We have no alternative; we must meet the enemy in combat, and destroy the satanic greed and

---

2. Psalms 55, 7.

diabolical cruelty of those who seek to up-root every vestige of human freedom and every semblance of divine justice. Peace is the aim of every duty which you are asked to perform, the motive for which you are asked to face each danger, and the dream of every person whose prayers follow you wherever your duty may carry you. The eyes of humanity-in-chains are upon you, and may the blessings of God rest upon you, and may He bring you all back safely to us.

PEACE WILL BE THE VICTOR

Sermon preached on July 24, 1943, at Dow Field, Maine

A LL OF us are agreed on the single yet all-embracing idea that motivates every American, be he in uniform or not, in this great historical crisis. You and I alike feel the momentousness of the situation through the realization that ours is not a war for self-aggrandizement or vain glory. We are not engaged in this tremendous war effort because of some dispute over territory. It is not even a question, as some consider it, of national honor. We are not inspired by grandiose dreams of self glorification, trade advantages, or other economic, political, or nationalistic considerations. This is a war of ideas and ideals, in which we seek to secure for our children and children's children, the blessings of peace and contentment. In the Biblical portion of this week, there is a similar significant situation in which the blessing of peace is vouchsafed through the medium of warlike action.

Phineas, the son of Eliezer, Ha Cohen, was singled out for divine recognition and gratitude because of his devotion and self-sacrifice in a critical hour. He saved the honor of Israel, and halted the growth and stopped the spread of a virulent and moral poison that menaced the camp of Israel and threatened it with spiritual suffocation and moral degeneracy. Much as it was distasteful to him to wield a dagger, the prompt action of the Priest saved his people from untold grief and enabled them to continue their march toward the land of promise and hope. And yet it is worth to note and very important to remember that when God honored Phineas, He did not reward him with a promise and assurance that all his descendants would become heroic soldiers. On the con-

(145)

trary while recognizing the tremendous importance of
his valorous deed, He rewarded him with a promise of
peace. As we read in the Weekly Portion;

"Therefore, speak unto him sayeth the Lord, behold, I
give him My covenant of peace."[1] What a magnificent
summation of all the dreams and visions that well up in
our hearts and souls when we think of the sacrifices of
war and of the beauty of peace. More specifically stated
—God speaks to us as he spoke to Phineas then; My son,
you took up arms and braved a treacherous foe in defense of decency and morality. You are offering, on the
altar of your people's love, all the dearest possessions
that life can hold out. In return for this, I promise you
and those that come after you, that my highest reward
of deepest appreciation will be a guarantee, that out of
your distressing experiences of war will come the promise
of a lasting peace. We in our time can ask for no more,
nay, it is the sum and substance of our fondest dreams.
We hope that our leaders and the leaders of mankind will
reward the selfless devotion, the boundless enthusiasm,
the supreme idealism and the unquestioned integrity of
America's splendid armed forces, by bringing unto them
and unto their children and their children's children, the
promise that since this horrible war was forced upon
us, we who take our mission with the sincere idealism of
Phineas, will be heralded anew with the prophetic
promise:

> "My covenant was with him, life and peace and I
> gave them to him for the fear wherewith he feared
> Me, and because of My Name he had dread."[2]

---

1. Numbers 41, 12.
2. Malachai 2, 5.

THE PAST THAT GUIDES US

Preached at Dow Field, July 31, 1943 by
RABBI ABRAHAM A. KELLNER

ALL OF us have a great deal of admiration for men of vision—people who have the foresight and courage to stride into new fields of endeavor, to explore unknown regions, to search the skies for the mysteries of creation, and to speculate intuitively about the unknown glories that man may achieve. There are times and seasons, however, when we must look backward instead of forward, when we must lean upon the past rather than the future and seek sustaining strength from yesterday, before we tackle the problems of tomorrow.

There are indeed people who label as weak those who are unable to decide their course in attempting to adjust themselves to the two directions alluded to above. Often these people go even further and level the callous charge that whilst life and the march of civilization impels us to look ahead, to march forward, and to institute progress, religion glories only in the accomplishments of the past, recalling continually the occurrences that were significant in the life of our forebears.

In a detached sense, it is true that the watch-word of our faith, particularly during the three weeks of lamentation which we count at present, is "Return Ye Erring Sons". This seeming contradiction is easily resolved, however, when we probe deeper into the mainsprings of our religious experience, and guide our actions in the present by the lessons gained from the failures of the past. The Biblical portion which is set aside for the Sabbath recounts the wanderings and travels of our

(147)

11

forefathers in the desert. It also is the closing chapter
of the fourth book of Moses which concerns itself a great
deal with the travels and travails of that desert generation which had knocked hopefully at the gates of the
promised lands. We read that Moses recounts in infinite, minute detail the story of these wanderers, and
carefully recites about the places in which they so-
journed, the communities which they visited, the problems they encountered, and the tribulations with which
they were faced. Significantly enough, these historical
facts were set down with minute consideration before
these charges of Moses were able to enter the Holy Land.
It is clearly established therefore that our great law-
giver sought to weave a careful pattern of historical
events and also to preserve them, that they might serve
as a guide for his charges in solving the perplexing problems with which they were to be faced. The major note
that recurs ever and anon in the Mosaic recital is the
reminder that their wanderings were the blue prints of
a Divine Plan, and that these wanderings should so
shape the future course of historical development that
it would fit into the heavenly plan of a commonwealth in
a kingdom of priests, where a holy nation would aim for
perfection and spiritual ennoblement.

We who are privileged to be members of the present
generation of Americans, have a great deal in common
with those ancient Hebrews whose lives were thus summed up before the realization of their age-old goal. We
too see the dim outlines of our Promised Land and with
the turn of war's fortune in our favor, we perceive,
partly if not fully, the pattern of future events in the
making of which we have such a noteworthy share. It
is well that we too should review the history of this
nation's tribulations as we prepare to enter the promised
land which a righteous peace will hold forth for us. We
too will find that not only was the early history of our

country fashioned after the exploits of Biblical heroes, but that our forefathers on this continent also envisioned a commonwealth where the law of God was manifest and just, and saintly human conduct would be the basic foundation of society.

I remember a story I once read from the pen of an American magazine-writer who had had an audience with one of the former rulers of Brazil. In it he told how this august personality compared the natural resources and potential wealth of our country with that of his own, and wanted to find why the standard of living was so much higher in our own United States than in his country, though his country, too, had untold possibilities of wealth and sustenance. After advancing several suggestions toward the solution of the problem, he finally concluded that our ancestors came to North America to find God, while his forebears were actuated by the desire to find gold. That, he concluded, is why we, here in the United States, have both.

This inspirational message should serve as an ever potent reminder to all of us that the early founders of America sought God, and were propelled by that desire to seek happiness in a new world. We who are called upon to explore many continents and fight on many seas, should bear that lesson in mind and in consequence thereof, we, too, will achieve honor for our land, glory for our God, and happiness for humanity.

OUT OF THE ASHES OF YESTERDAY

Preached at the Friday Night Services of the Army Specialized
Training Unit, University of Maine, August 6, 1943

THE Shabbos which we observe tonight and tomorrow
has become invested with the holiness of sorrowful
remembrances, since it precedes the ninth day of
Ab. The destruction of our Holy Temple, the loss of
the Jewish State, and numerous other tragic occurrences
in our unhappy history, are commemorated on this day.
Strangely enough, most people set aside the days of
their victory, of national glory, to be observed and cele-
brated; we, on the other hand, observe with most me-
ticulous care the day which marks the most catastrophic
defeat ever suffered by us. The reasons for this are not
far to seek. First, we are contented with the knowledge
that ours was a just cause and that the mighty legions
of Rome, who laid waste the hallowed edifices and Temple
Heights, did not necessarily represent right by the apparent advantage of their might. Our whole way of
life or modus vivendi that has been observed by the
Jewish people throughout their long past, has always
been predicated on the sincere conviction that they
would rather lose on the side of righteousness than win
with the blood of innocents on their hands.

I remember having preached a Thanksgiving Sermon
in 1938 immediately after the horrible pogroms in Germany. Some sincere but terrified people asked me what
a Jew can be thankful for at such a time and I told them
that it is with the deepest gratitude that we approach
the Throne of the Almighty Lord to express our thank-
fulness that we were among those who were hurt rather
than among the ones who were inflicting pain upon their
fellow men. If a choice had to be made, I am satisfied

(150)

that my people would rather suffer the most horrible visitations of history than have to stand at the Bar of Justice at some future time and answer for the crimes and monstrosities committed against our fellow men.

Even more important is the fact that when we Jews commemorate the sad occurrences of Tisha B'ab, we do so with the unshakeable faith and unyielding hope that a bright day will follow the endless silence of the long dark night, even as light appeared on that first day of creation, when the pattern had been set and the norm established. It seems to be characteristic of the history and destiny of the Jew, because, as we experience the coming of the night, we are certain that we shall be there to greet the rise of the new dawn when we shall hear the Command of God once again: "And the Lord said, Let there be Light."[1]

Characteristic also, of this indomitable will to live, is the comment of our sages that: **B'tisha b'aav nalod moashiach.** On the day of our greatest sorrows, the redeemer was born. Out of the ashes of yesterday, that buried the hopes of Israel, rises the glow of a quenchless fire that illuminates the path of our wanderings and sheds its warm rays in the cruel age of barbarism. This pillar of fire, which was born when calamity reigned supreme, enables us to face the uncertain future with serenity and quiet determination.

In our own day, we are privileged to see that that which has held true in the history of Israel is true, even to a greater measure, in the history of our greatly beloved U. S. We, too, entered this war on the day of a great disaster, when the initial set-backs and early defeats, suffered at the hands of a then numerically larger

---

1. Genesis 1, 3.

foe, crushed the hopes of those whose judgment was blurred by the events passing in review. Those of us whose character was made of stronger fibre, never wavered for a moment. We did not falter when Bataan fell, and we were certain of eventual victory when the heroes of Corregidor laid down their arms. The lessons of history are on our side, and no matter how deep the disappointments were at first, we marched forward with unflinching loyalty and undaunted courage for justice and righteousness. We who are warriors in the battle for Godliness know that out of the ashes of yesterday will rise the fire of a victorious tomorrow.

RELIGION'S VOICE IN CHANGING
THE WORLD

Preached over Columbia's Church of the Air,
August 22, 1943

A S THE news from the global battle zones continues in an encouraging vein, American public opinion, ever a potent force in our Democracy, focuses the searchlight of investigation upon the problems of the peace to come.

It is understood even by poorly informed observers that profound and far-reaching changes in the political, economic, and social landscape of the world are in the throes of creation. Distinguished American and World leaders speak of the problems affecting humanity in terms of One World, Two Way Passage, Warning to the West, and other studies of a serious nature that seek to encompass the perplexities of mankind in this fateful hour. The forces of religion, although wholly in agreement with the pressure of timely innovations, nevertheless speak to the leaders of mankind on a note of reminder that all the programs proposed, all the solutions advanced, and all the panaceas presented, are by themselves insufficient, and lacking in the cohesive mortar that must go into building-up the structure of peace. The efforts so far expended concern themselves indeed with the question of geographic boundaries, the problems of economic self-sufficiency, the perplexities of political prudence; however, they do not take into consideration the significance of the spiritual values which must serve as the basis for every plan that envisages a changing world as a result of this war.

(153)

It is well that Americans consider the spiritual aspects of making the world over, and invoke the spirit of religion in the high places of authority where the plans will be made and the projects considered to establish a pattern for a more harmonious universe. From its very inception, the United States was nurtured on religious idealism and fostered by Biblical inspiration. The descendents of the Revolutionary heroes who emblazoned on the Liberty Bell the deathless refrain from Holy Writ, "And Ye shall proclaim liberty in the land unto all the inhabitants thereof",[1] have indeed a righteous demand when they petition the powers-that-be for a guarantee that the hallowed spirit of religion should not be stifled at the Council Tables where decisions affecting the political climate of the earth will be made.

No suggestion is entertained here to have high ecclesiastical dignitaries present at the Peace Conference. It is for the spirit of religion that we plead rather than for its symbols or for the authorities representing them. The plea is made for the religious idealism that preaches the essential dignity of man, man who is crowned with the attribute of having been created in the Image of God, "For in His Image hath He made him."[2] The idealism which proclaims the immortal precept "Love thy neighbor as thyself"[3] and places mankind upon a pedestal declaring each man to be an equal of his fellowman, is that spirit which does not recognize the artificially created differences of class or the mechanically devised distinctions of creed and the ruthlessly imposed myths of race.

The spirit of religion that we should like to see enthroned high in the values of the peace-makers is that quenchless idealism that is the lief motif of the Declara-

1. Leviticus XXV, 10.
2. Genesis I, 27.
3. Leviticus XIX, 18.

tion of Independence. This manifesto declares the Sovereignty of God over all the earth, and rings out in clear tones the concept of the inalienable right of all men to life, liberty, and the pursuit of happiness. The resistless spirit of freedom surging from the lifeblood of a religiously inclined nation enable the early settlers of these beloved United States to bring about, by the Grace of God, those wondrous achievements which have made our country the cynosure of all eyes. Feeling secure in his faith in God, convinced that the Creator and Ruler of the Universe brought this planet into existence for the benefit and salvation of man, the early pioneer proceeded to subdue the primeval forest, plow the golden fields, and build the magnificent network of roads that enabled their progeny to people the land with happy and industrious inhabitants, from the rockbound coast of the Atlantic to the golden shores of the Pacific.

Our path to world happiness and security is clear if we only abide by these principles enunciated by our forebears. Indeed, we cannot do better than to take as our own pattern for world reconstruction the blueprints employed by the Creator Himself, when He called this world into being. The wise men of the Talmud list the tools and implements used in the formation of the world. They could still effectively serve those designing a New World.

> "With ten things was the world created", taught Rabbi Zutra ben Tubia: "Wisdom and Understanding, Knowledge and Strength, Rebuke and Might, Righteousness and Justice, Mercy and Compassion."[4]

First then under consideration is Chochmoh—Wisdom. And Wisdom to us would manifest itself in the concept

4. Talmud, Chaggigal 12a.

of King David that the wisdom needed in refreshing a battered world is

"The Beginning of Wisdom, Which is the Fear of God."[5]

Godliness, superimposed upon the peace planners, would surely start the March of Progress off on a smooth path. With Wisdom as a signpost, the world must be guided by an understanding of human nature. A secure knowledge of the problems of mankind and the strength to deal with recalcitrant trouble-makers must be cultivated. Rebuke and Might are the, next two attributes with which the leaders of mankind must endow themselves in order to mete out justice and punishment to those criminals who have brought this war into being, and to control the pressure groups who even now are planning the next war. Over and above all other considerations the creed of Righteousness and Justice, and the one of Mercy and Compassion, must be developed and spread among the men and women of this earth, so that they will earn and know the meaning of a full and rich life.

Surely the people of Israel, who were the first to suffer the tyrant's lash, do not advocate a policy of revenge. They ask only that justice be done for their people who first taught an unwilling world the primary lessons in Justice and Mercy. America too, when called upon to make her sacrifices and offer her contributions upon the altar of human freedom, is willing and ready to do her share without thought of profit or gain. Our nation is not anxious to benefit in a territorial sense from this welter of human unhappiness and misery. We will not ask for punitive indemnities. The people of this country, however, will ask that in order to compensate in a small measure for the bloody sacrifices given by them,

---

5. Psalms III, 10.

the principle basic to all great religions should dominate the deliberations of those upon whose shoulders the great responsibilities rest, and who are in charge of the fate of mankind.

At this time, when we are in the throes of a fearsome dream come true, and the ghosts of the darkest evil cast their sinister shadows over a humanity dismembered and at war with itself, it is the vital task of America that its free voice should be heard and heeded. It is the voice of a nation in whose soul there is no vindictiveness, no revenge, but the overwhelming desire to extinguish the blaze which fans the Passions of hate and which threatens the ending of this civilization. Our heroic men in the many branches of the Armed Services seek **victory,** not conquest; their aims are for **peace,** not tyranny. They do not have the lust for bloodshed that is heard in the marching songs of those who foisted intellectual nihilism upon mankind and who sought to spread spiritual anarchy over the face of the globe.

Our task is obvious. It is our duty to light the way to the road that will lead humanity to the high plateaus of world peace. To do this, we will have the primary objective of ridding this world of ours of the abominations forced upon us by the hordes of satan who stirred up this fiery holocaust and who polluted the moral atmosphere of this earth. If we unite our efforts, if we try to build upon the charred ruins of our society a better integrated and more enduring fellowship of nations, we will find ourselves embarking upon a great adventure, an adventure into the field of human relations where the outcome is of such glorious promise that free men will willingly stake their all to attain it.

GREATEST AND BEST

Preached for the Naval Personnel at Congregation Gomley
Chesed, Portsmouth, Va., November 5, 1943

IN THIS moment of rare exultation when the inspiring chant of Sabbath Eve melodies bring back to us memories of our dear ones everywhere, I want to say a word about the feeling of pride every American takes in the wondrous achievement of your branch of service, the United States Navy. Yet, in the very same moment, there is a need for a note of warning lest the glory in your attainments be expressed in strictly materialistic terms.

There would be little for a Rabbi to take pride in, if all our boasts were to be exhausted in recounting the number of vessels of every description which daily join our Fleet, or in recounting the tonnage, or the striking power, or the all around superiority of these vessels. We would rather think of you as messengers of mercy, who protect our boys on their trips to and from the battle-fronts of the world. Our pride in you is expressed by the feeling that you are agents of righteousness who stake everything, including life itself, to help remove the blight of tyranny from the earth. You can indeed glory in your deeds when they are considered in the light of the world's sorrow which brought your magnificent organization into being.

The Scriptural lesson of our Sabbath contains a most timely reminder that mere imposing size, greatness of quantity, and vast limits, do not in themselves indicate a blessed state of affairs. The portion speaks of the early experiences of our grandsire, Abraham, who incidentally gave us our historic appelation of Hebrew,[1]

---

1. Genesis 14, 13. See Rashi.

by crossing the great waters of the East not unlike your tasks of today. The Lord in speaking to him assured him: "I will make thy name great."[2] Lest this greatness be interpreted in mere physical strength, in sheer power and influence, Holy Writ hastens to add: **Vheyeh brocho**—"And Ye shall be for a Blessing."[3] His might and power, his strength and influence will be employed for the good and will be beneficial to all humanity. In strange contrast and evident contradistinction is the tale of an earlier generation, members of which also had grandiose dreams and who envisioned as the object of their goal an imposing tower of immense magnitude, the greatest, the most stupendous, and by far the most colossal venture of their times. In reading the Scriptural account of their enterprise, one finds no evidence that any desire dwelt in their hearts to turn this boisterous adventure to public good. Their sole concern and singular driving force was expressed in the egotistical self glorification: **V'naase lono shem**—"To make unto ourselves a name."[4] There are nations in the world today whose wicked designs you are defeating, who, like the builders of the Tower of Babel, sought to arrogate unto themselves name and fame built on blood and destruction; they dreamed in terms of world conquest, and not only hurled their satanic challenge to the peace loving nations of the earth, but, in their blinded fury they dared imagine that no power, even that of Heaven, could stop their strutting arrogance. Their purpose like that of the men of Babel will end in utter confusion and rout, whilst you, whose greatness is measured in the Abrahamic concept of blessed influence will bring light and humanity and blissful tranquility to a world so sadly in need of peace.

---

2. Genesis 12, 2.
3. Ibid.
4. Ibid., 11, 4.

THE GLORY OF THE IMPERFECT

Preached at Sampson Naval Base
Sunday, March 26, 1944

IN A very short time we shall once again celebrate the glorious Spring Festival of Passover which will bring back to our minds the heroic character of Moses, our great master. Moses, our great law-giver, like the valiant men of the United States Navy, came into prominence upon the mighty waters.

It is of the history of Moses that I want to speak this morning, thereby drawing a parallel from his life that has important bearing upon the events of our times. There are many people who are greatly disheartened when they are prevented from completing a task once begun. In their hasty judgment these individuals fail to realize that an effort honestly made, an attempt whole-heartedly embarked upon, a goal relentlessly pursued, or an ambition unyieldingly sought after, bears its own fruit even when not reached in its entirety. The Talmud tells the familiar story of the man who was planting an exotic tree which does not yield fruit for seventy years. Upon being questioned by a passing stranger as to whether he expects to live long enough to eat the fruit of this tree, he replied:

> "Coming into the world, I already found such trees that some of my forbears planted for me. I, in turn, must plant the seed that will yield fruit for my children or children's children."[1]

This statement, most convincingly sums up the argument that even when success is not immediate, the goal must be pursued.

---

1. Talmud, Taanith, XXIIIa.

Moses had as his goal the desire to lead the people of Israel into the Promised Land. That ambition he failed to achieve. Does that in any manner lessen the glory of his numerous other magnificent achievements? Of course and emphatically no!

Similarly a generation before us, brave men of America sailed forth to try to establish lasting peace in the world. That exalted ideal was not realized in their life-time, but this does not by one iota diminish the glory of their dream and the grandeur of their venture. Even in its imperfect glory, their quenchless idealism will shine through the ages as a heroic example for their progeny.

The example of the Vermont stone-cutter who labored unceasingly on a particular slab of granite should be remembered. Each day he smote the stone, and then, one day, a stranger came by and with only one mighty stroke sheared the stone asunder. It was not the strength of the stranger that caused the breaking up of the stone; it was in reality the successive strokes administered by the patient Vermont cutter that bore the fruit; it was due to the cutter's constant and persistent endeavors that success was achieved. Just so our concepts of lasting peace and good will are due to the persistent and patient efforts of our forebears who planted the seeds of liberty which are flowering in our time.

The Rabbis of the Mishna summed up this philosophy by assuring those who timidly would avoid a task of whose completion they are not certain. **V'lo olecho hamlocho l'igmor**—"It is not expected of you to complete all tasks in their entirety."[2] Your is not the responsibility to reach perfection in all your aims; this, however, does not justify anyone's shirking his duty, nor does it absolve anyone from doing his finest, think-

---

2. Aboth II, 21.

ing his highest, and feeling his deepest when historic
tasks beckon.   **V'lo ato ben-chorin l'hivotel mimenoh.**[3]
We must forever expand our finest energies on the anvil
of the universe where the star of tomorrow's hope is
beaten into form by the sanctified efforts of successive
generations who in their time have written large the
epic of their days, just as you write today, indelibly upon
the pillars of history, your magnificent contributions
toward the age-old dream of a world ever at peace.

---

3. Ibid.

CROSSING OUR BRIDGES SAFELY

Preached at the Syracuse Army Air Base, September 5, 1944

W E MEET tonight in a fellowship of prayer, and mine is the privilege to address you, my fellow Americans, on the special significance of this observance of Labor Day.

On this day, America pauses to honor our men and women who are the soldiers of the army of Labor. It is these soldiers of production who have done so remarkably well in building up the Arsenal of Democracy that is America. It takes little search in our Holy Writ to find adequate ground for singing the praises of this mighty army of producers. Throughout the story of Creation, the Almighty is constantly referred as to a Doer, Maker, and Creator. The Biblical Law and the stories of the lives of our great men are replete with the achievements which their efforts produced. Betzalel, builder of the Sanctuary, is a sterling example of the might of Labor. King Solomon was the architect of the Holy Temple, and there is Ezra who built on the ruins of the past, a new and more marvelous Jerusalem.[1]

II

These thoughts bring to mind another and more often overlooked element that makes possible the march of progress, and, we hope, ultimate victory. A quaint and popular allegory in the Midrash will serve to illustrate the meaning of this other element I speak of. We remember from our childhood the beautiful story that was

---

1. Haggai, 2, 9.

told us about the future Messianic time, when all the peoples of the earth would be brought to the banks of a great water; upon their arrival, they would be confronted with the problem of crossing this expanse, and they would be offered the choice of two bridges, one constructed of steel; the other of paper. The wicked people of the earth will be forced to cross on the mighty bridge of steel, but when they are half-way across, it will collapse under the terrible load of their sinfulness and iniquity. The righteous of the world will make their way across the bridge of paper, but lo and behold, it will bear their weight with ease, and they will all arrive safely on the other side.

Whatever one may think of the practical aspects of this prophecy, one's attention should be called to a bit of contemporary history. As the fearsome hosts of our enemies descended upon the Low Countries, as they conquered Scandinavia, subdued France, and over-ran the Balkans, it seemed a sheer impossibility to stop their ravaging trek over their prostrate neighbors. The power of evil and the minions of loathsome darkness had their mighty bridge of steel ready for the final crossing of the English Channel and were preparing eventually to make an onslaught on these our own shores. We heard the terrifying tales of their vaunted armor, and we read the descriptions of their murderous stuka dive-bombers. We saw pictures of the horror and desolation accompanying their blitz attacks, and we recoiled at the fiendish cruelty of their submarine warfare. The world was made aware of the power of their arrogant Panzer units and their death-dealing monster tanks. Our own armor was woefully weak and we knew that when pitted against the strength of our enemies, we were justified in being dismayed and frightened. But there were other elements in our favor besides the magnitude of strength. Our Democracy had forces with which the harbingers of evil did not reckon. Aye, my friends, let us remember our fervent prayers and supplications; let us recall the Bridge of Paper which our people crossed as we held clutched tightly to our breasts our prayer-books and our Torahs, intoning our deathless reaffirmation:

"From the Depths have I cried unto Thee, O Lord."
"Even though I walk in the Valley of the Shadow of Death, I shall fear no evil."

The people of England had little in the way of Bridges of Steel, but they had the faith of their fathers. In the darkest days of the blitz, they repaired to their stricken cathedrals, there to declare to an admiring world, their unflagging devotion and faith in Him Who was their Protector in Ages Past.

Our people had nought but the hallowed bridges of paper, washed by the ancient tears of oppression, carrying the Word of God upon which to pin their hope and trust. But these filmsy bridges always stood up under the strongest stress and strain, and were the means by which our people have always safely crossed the engulfing depths of adversity.

III

In the final analysis, we are implored never to forget in the impending hour of triumph, that we are waging a war, not of aggression or self-aggrandizement, but a war to finally determine whether or not the principles of Justice and Equality for all mankind can really be made to be the foundation-stones of our civilization. We are fighting to defend Godliness and the ideals of humanity. It is faith in our Creator that has given us the inspiration, fortitude, and endurance, to stand up under the

cruel blows of war. This Divine bedrock was strengthened by the stupendous effort of the Home Front, and it
is now, thank God, being brought to fruition by the
colossal and heroic efforts of our boys and girls in uniform. As we chart the course of the coming years, and
as we explore the paths of future progress, we shoud do
as our forebears did upon entering the Land of Promise.
We, too, should offer up the first fruits of our labor as a
Thanksgiving. We must work so that the principles of
Freedom and Liberty which we have labored to achieve
shall become a reality to the oppressed peoples of the
earth, so that they too may share of the goodliness, thereof. Then, and only then, we shall never have fear of the
evil Bridges of Steel.

THE WHY AND HOW OF GIVING

U. J. A. Address—Syracuse Orthodox Council, April 11, 1943

W E MEET tonight under the shadow of a great World War and in the expectation of the festival of Passover which will be with us in a few days. Of the many explanations, commentaries, and interpretations with which the story of our liberation is embellished, none is as important as the injunction of our sages that we ought to consider the incidents of our ancient past as if they were occurrences of the present. The Jew indeed does not look upon Abraham, Isaac, Jacob, Moses, and Aaron as belonging to an ancestral past, nor as part and parcel of a dim and remote memory. We see in these patriots and law-givers real and vivid personalities who speak to us in the present and encourage us for the future by the inspiration of their accomplishment. Our sages thus instruct us, and we read in the Haggaddah: "In every generation a Jew must look upon himself as though he had just departed form the land of Egypt".[1] The Passover message is incomplete if it merely implies the recitation of ancient glories; its significance should be reflected in our daily lives as history is known to repeat itself.

It is therefore one of the basic errors of most American Jewish fund-raising campaigns that they address themselves to the people of America with an abstract plea for some unfortunate sufferers in a distant land. These pleas instead should be predicated upon the conviction that it is a part of the Jewish whole that suffers, a limb, so to say, of the body politic of world Jewry, a part of our own Jewish entity, blood of our blood, flesh

---

1. Talmud, Pesachim CXVI, b.

of our flesh. Let us consider this error in the light of an individual who suffers from a foot ailment, or a toothache, or a disease of the mouth; he does not need to make an appeal to his heart and soul to take care of the ailing member of his body. Neither should we have to plead with one part of the Jewish body to please have mercy and extend the means of healing to the ailing portion of the Jewish nation.

Last Shabbos we read in the prophetic portion of the week the ever romantic episode in the lives of Jonothan and David, of their pledge of fidelity and the sweet sorrow of their parting. Their period in Jewish history was crowded with numerous incidents of dramatic intensity, but none as tragic as the delusion of King Saul which prompted him to challenge Fate in his attempt to bar the path of David and prevent him from reaching the kingship of Israel. As matters grew steadily worse for the annointed ruler of the Hebrews, he sought desperate measures to re-establish himself in the eyes of God and to strengthen the tottering foundation of his once glorious throne. In one despairing moment, we read in the Second Book of Samuel, King Saul disguised himself and, accompanied by a faithful officer of his guard, he implored the witch of Ain Dor to bring up out of the grave the spirit of his departed mentor, Samuel— a practice, incidentally, which King Saul had previously forbidden under pain of death. After much hesitancy, the sorceress agreed and good the vision of Samuel's presence was apparent in the room. Saul appealed to Samuel for aid in his fight for reinstatement into glory. The Scriptures quote Samuel's reproving reply:

> "Why hast thou disturbed me, to bring me up from the grave?"[2]

Those sad words of a departed friend echo the disillu-

---

2. Samuel I, XXVIII, 15.

sionment of a lifetime and the castigations of a dis-
carded counsellor. Samuel could be heard with bitter
lament perhaps as follows: "Saul, King of the Hebrews,
I spent many precious years in guiding you through the
complicated labyrinth and through the maze of intric-
acies that had to be traversed by those who aspire to
rule; I gave you the best of my life, the best guidance of
my ability, the finest counsel of my intelligence. Am I
not entitled to my rest? Why? Why? Why? do you
knock on my grave to disturb my silent sleep and to call
me up to this world again." Such must have been the
response of Samuel. We can well imagine that if the
mangled bodies of our fellow Jews of Europe could speak
to us, they too, would complain with the lament of
Samuel. Have they not done enough for American
Jewry? Did they not supply the sinews for the spiritual
structure that went into the building of the American
Jewish community? Are we not everlastingly indebted
to them for the enduring contributions they made to the
cultural education and religious strength of American
Jewry?

Why? they ask, Why? Why? must we call their now
blessed souls from their graves to obtain the funds for
the rescue and maintenance of those still alive? Are the
Jews of America so callous? Have they grown so indiffer-
ent that we must actually rattle the bones of the victims
of Hitlerism before their hearts soften and they assume
their share in the saving of the remnants of our folk?
I appeal to the Jews of this community to think in terms
of Israel's history and to envisage the efforts of reconstruction which the agencies of mercy, created by the
vision of some American Jews, proposed to carry
through, if only they are provided with the funds essential for their labors.

There is an ancient legend told about a mythical debate

between a spider and a bee, each arguing that it is the more important creature. The spider recounted an incident of antiquity that when King David, while escaping from the minions of Saul, found refuge in a deserted cave, a spider, see his predicament, wove a thick covering of webbed hair over the mouth of the cave. When the soldiers approached the cave, they turned aside remarking that the cave was uninhabited for a long time because of the spider web. "Thus," said the spider triumphantly, "it was one of my kind that saved King David from capture and certain death." "Possibly so", answered the bee "but I will not go so far as to justify my superior existence. I help in preparing delightful honey whose taste sweetens the life of many people today." My friends, I will not appeal to you in the name of Israel's great past, though I could. I merely want you to remember that your generous contribution may sweeten the lives of harassed and terrified little children whose years have been embittered by the anguish of separation, loneliness, and exile. Wipe away those tears, heal their wounds, and sweeten the last days of weary old people whose only crime has been that they are Jews.

U. J. A. ADDRESS AT BRITH SHALOM DINNER

Norfolk, Va., November 3, 1943

IT IS a privilege to speak before such a representative and distinguished group of my fellow Jews who are banded together in a great Order whose very name reminds us of the covenant of our people and the glorified ideal of Peace, which, indeed, is the historic mission of Israel. The combination of noble purpose of **Zshedakah**, which actuates your presence tonight together with the resistless striving for peace that is the motif of your organization, will enable you to hasten effectively the coming of the day foretold by the prophet Isaiah: "And the work of Tzodokoh shall be peace; and the effect of rightousness; security."—**V'hoyoh maasei hatzdokoh sholam**[1] because you work for sweet charity and holy purposes; it will bring nearer the fervently awaited day when peace will once more reign supreme.

I am also greatly pleased to visit once more this historic vicinity in this great Dominion State, the Commonwealth of Virginia, where the basic foundation of genuine Americanism was conceived, and which gave to our country so many of the architects that helped fashion and design our great democracy. But the wonderful growth of the United States from its humble beginning is not as astonishing as may appear on the surface. Those of us who are parents have at one time or another experienced a genuine thrill, a wonderful sensation and a magnificent feeling as we watched for the first time our blessed little offspring take a halting and faltering step. It is one of the glories of parenthood to watch our chil-

---

1. Isaiah, 32, 17.

dren try their wings for the first time. But that is a
natural course and it is in the normal order of events
that growing babes and developing children take their
initial steps and gradually acquire the use of their limbs
to the fullest capacity. Such is the history of these
United States, and if we wonder at its marvelous growth,
we must remember that, having been endowed by Providence with fertile lands, luxuriant forests, immense
mineral deposits, majestic rivers, and untold wealth, on,
above and below its surface, it was only natural that
given wise leadership and patient guidance, this infant
nation which was conceived in liberty, should grow into
the giant which it is today.

It is a far different story, however, when we consider
the case of an old person, wearied by age and broken by
the toil of the years. Let us assume that this exhausted
individual falls victim to a paralytic attack and then by
the grace of God and medical attention, patient treat-
ment and persevering care, this invalid is enabled once
again to slowly effect the use of his limbs; imagine the
thrill of his family, his children and his grandchildren
when they see this bruised and battered grandparent
take his first steps by himself once again. Such, my
friends, is the case of aged and wearied Israel.
We who appeal to you today to save the remnants of
our people's martyrs, speak for an old and wearied
people, who has suffered a most destroying malady of
persecution and battering bruises, a malady which has
sought to exterminate them completely. We ask you
to remember our suffering brethren across the seas and
to help provide the means which will enable this paralyzed
body of a people to be healed of its wounds so that it
too can take once more its first faltering steps toward
freedom and happiness. If the American Jewish Community rises to the occasion imposed upon it by this
tragedy, it will effectively cause the reestablishment of

the shattered fragments of a broken people into an integrated and cohesive entity.

There may be some among us who are wearied of the constant appeal for funds and the continual reminder to their sense of loyalty. Frankly as I rode down from New York today, travelling in a most uncomfortable coach, crowded to capacity, I too, felt a momentary discomfort and questioned the wisdom of my decision in leaving my home and family to travel this long distance for the sake of this appeal. Then an old Arabian proverb came to my mind; it speaks of a man who always complained because he did not have shoes until he met a person who did not have feet. My friends, how dare we utter even one word of complaint if our good allotments are slightly restricted? Think of the millions who are daily dying of a slow starvation. If our children are asked to bear arms, to leave home, and to brave a thousand dangers, compare them with the millions who are the victims and not the ultimate victors. Compare them with those who are shot down in cold blood and slaughtered without mercy, with not a chance for protection and defense. What right would I have to complain of a day's travel in a comfortless train when I think of the many thousands who were packed worse than beasts into the death wagons of Poland and driven off to die in a most horrible inferno ever known to man?

Present here with me tonight is a distinguished colleague and honored spiritual leader in Israel, Rabbi Greenfield, of your neighboring town of Portsmouth. He told me a moment ago a moving tale of a Jewish sailor who came to the president of a Synagogue and asked him for the loan of a Sefer Torah which he and his shipmates wanted to use during the recent holiday period. When this blue jacket noticed some reluctance on the part of the congregational leader, he told him: "I know what is worrying you. You want to know what will happen to the Sefer Torah if the ship should be sunk. Frankly, I do not know, but I guarantee you one thing— if I come off the boat alive, the Sefer Torah will come off with me."

Friends, we have been blessed in that we were privileged to depart through the medium of parents from the blazing ship, from the burning hell known as Europe. Are we as determined, as resolute, as that brave lad of the United States Navy? Will you allow the blazing sinking ship of humanity to carry into the depths of the seas the remnants of our people, our blood brothers and sisters? Or will you contribute in a manner most generous to the cause that represents the salvaging of what may remain of our brethren from the horrible butcher of Nazidom? Will you help in strengthening the foundations of the Jewish community in the Holy Land? And will you support the appeal which seeks to save the Sefer Torah, the soul of the Jew in these trying times?

THOSE WHO DIED IN VAIN

Preached at the Memorial Services and U. J. A. Rally,
Congregation Agudus Achim, Kingston, N. Y.,
September 12, 1943

A T THE time the dreaded Chmelnitsky pogroms ravaged and decimated Russo-Polish Jewry close to three hundred years ago, a remarkable incident took place in the market place of Warsaw soon after the atrocities ceased. The wealthiest Jew of the province who apparently salvaged his fortune, converted his assets into gold and caused it to be announced throughout the city, that he would pay a golden ruble for the body of every dead Jew and two golden rubles for every Jew brought to him alive. The rabble who had a day before followed the inciting murderers, now became anxious to defend those Jews still in the realm of the living. The benefactor of his people achieved two noble purposes: He was able to make arrangements for appropriate burial rites for those who had perished by the fury of the mob, while at the same time, he could insure sanctuary for those who were still alive though in danger.

This dramatic episode in the history of our people's martyrdom is tragically timely tonight when we gather to shed a tear and give utterance to the soul-searing anguish which corrodes our hearts and very beings. It is not even our sorrowful privilege to arrange for the burial ceremonies of our tortured kin. Their earthly remains lie in the mass graves of Poland, in those gase chambers and death-wagons which are the mute witnesses to history's shame. In our inarticulate misery, we must bemoan the massacre of those who did not have to die— some who were so young and helpless, who could have

(175)

been in the land of the living and could have felt the life blood coursing through their veins for many, many years. I am referring to those young people of Poland who were anxious, desirous and eager to emigrate to the Holy Land or to other places of refuge before the deluge of fire broke loose and hell on earth, became a stark and fearsome reality in central and eastern Europe. We like to recall with pride our contribution toward the upbuilding of Palestine through the settlement of the several hundred thousand Jews in that blessed land. We point with pride, to the three hundred thousand of our fellow Jews who entered the Holy Land since the advent of Hitlerism. These brands plucked from the burning fire are certainly our greatest consolation in this dark night of our horrible sorrow. The share of American Jewry in their deliverance will redound to the glory of our children for generations to come. But what will we answer at the Bar of Heavenly Justice when we will be confronted with the irrefutable evidence of our ability to have been able to do more, cancelled only by our unwillingness to do so in recent years. In the wake of the first World War, when terror and famine ravished the Jewish masses of Eastern Europe, thousands upon thousands begged for the chance and pleaded for the new opportunity in our sacred land. Those were the days when our hopes were not scuttled by infamous White Papers. That was the period when enthusiasm ran high over the bright prospects of an early Jewish Commonwealth on the hallowed soil of our people. There were also other avenues of escape and other channels of emigration such as to North and South America. The only thing that retarded their progress, restricted their advance, rescinded their hopes and restrained their desires, was their improverished condition and their utter inability to raise the necessary funds for their journey of liberation.

Tonight's services must include a soul-searching Viddui and a heart cleansing confession as we realize that so many could have been saved. They perished, perhaps because we waited, until the brutalities of barbaric Hitlerism reached their unspeakable heights, before we were willing to consider the possibility of giving until it hurts and even after it hurts. In my reservoir of tears, the ones that scald my eyes the fiercest, are those for the Jews who did not have to die and who could have been saved and I speak only of them, for whom we are responsible. Let mankind, if it has a conscience, answer its own indictment for permitting Hitlerism to run amuck and for its failure to restrain the terror when it still had the power. And for its failure even now, to employ effective means for the redemption of those who can be still snatched from the jaws of death.

Yesterday we read in our Synagogues the Sedra known as Shoftim which contains the divine admonition that "Justice, only Justice, shalt thou pursue."[1] This heavenly command has reference to the acts of the Judges, during the process of discharging their official duties. It underlines a major element in the all inclusive unity of Jewish life, whose connotations affect both the behavior of the individual as well as a universal moral principle, in denoting communal responsibility. It is a guarantee that an individual, though he be poor, down-trodden, and helpless, will be dealt with fairly and justly; and it implies the observances of social responsibilities in all their ramifications and with all their perplexities. The Torah concerns itself with the welfare and happiness of every individual as it seeks to cement the foundations of a social order whose enduring qualities perfect the fabric of our civilization.

A striking illustration of the aforementioned attitude

---

1. Deuteronomy: 16, 20.

is found in the concluding verses of that Biblical subdivision:

"If one is found slain in the land which the Lord thy God giveth thee to possess it, lying in the field and it be not known who had smitten him."[2] Biblical law proceeds to instruct the fact that the proximity of the nearest city be established and that the elders of that community must wash their hands clean of the charge of murder, exclaiming as follows:

"Our hands have not spilled this blood, and our eyes have not seen it."[3]

The Rabbis of the Talmud caught the apparent inconsistency of the ritual, and in indignant tones inquired:

"Would it enter anyone's mind to suspect that the elders of the community are murderers?"[4] They elucidate in answering their own query. The reference is thus made to sin of omission rather than to a crime of commission:

"We have not discharged him without food and victuals, without support and accompaniment."[5] Those in charge of the community were thus called upon to testify before God and man that the stranger and the homeless was not allowed to wander about without shelter and food; that even an unknown wanderer was accorded succor and protection. The responsibility enunciated here was especially severe about those who did not have to die and who could have been saved if the community had allotted to them the measure of protection and support enumerated in the laws of the Bible.

---

2. Ibid. 21, 1.
3. Ibid. 21, 7.
4. Talmud: Sotah 48b.
5. Idem.

If our remorse is so vast and our contrition so keen about the opportunity missed and the obligation neglected, how much greater should be our determination to help those where speedy and large-scale assistance can still be brought into play to salvage those remnants fleeing from the great world storm?

I am pleased to see such a wonderful turnout of Jewish women and I address myself to them with a pathetic plea and a heart-breaking supplication. You, as Mothers in Israel, know the meaning of compassionate love for one's offspring. Will you join the ranks of those angels of mercy through whose efforts and unlimited devotion the wounds are healed, the tears are dried, and the mourners are comforted? You women who know and understand values, will you inspire your men, and will you invite your fellow women to participate in the greatest bargain sale in history? In Festung Europa, there is a bargain basement for smart buyers where shrewd purchasers can pick up for a pittance human lives that are cheap on the market and debased in value. It is a discontinued line that we have there, because Hitler's Europe must become **Judenrein.** They are in broken sizes. They are little people who have aged before their time. They are the young people whose faces are lined, not with the soothing hands of the passing years but by the stark terror etched forever in their souls. They are an odd lot, indiscriminately containing the strong and weak, the learned and ignorant. They are mostly soiled merchandise whose virtue was defiled, whose sanctity was invaded, and whose purity was besmirched by the bloody touch of beasts walking about in the guise of humankind.

The gavel of the auctioneer bangs down on their broken bodies and it is your opportunity to choose whether or not you will allow the marauders of mankind

13

and decency to extinguish the last faint vestiges of
Jewish life in Europe. Or will you snatch them up at
the ridiculously cheap price offered to us? There are
29,000 or more unused certificates guaranteeing admission to the Holy Land. Regardless of the outcome of
the political battle waged about the infamous White
Paper, this number will be permitted to enter Palestine
as long as the funds are provided by American Jewry.
Your share in this great campaign is considerably higher
than the goal set for yourselves last year. It is still
nowhere near the tremendous potentialities which it
connotates. Yours is a simple choice. Remember they
no longer can choose! We by the Grace of God are here
safe. They are in danger! What is your decision?
What will your answer be? Won't you give them a
chance?

THE PRIMACY OF THE SPIRIT

Radio Address—Broadcast on January 2, 1944, Station WABY
Albany Ministerial Association

B Y PRESIDENTIAL proclamation and request, the people of America were urged to spend the first day of the calendar year or a part thereof in prayer and devotion, asking for the blessings of God above upon the efforts of our warriors. Thus we prayed, hoping that our prayers for a speedy and complete victory would soon be answered.

To one who has been nurtured upon the tenents of the Mosaic faith, this presidential request did not constitute a departure from established usage, for ever since the time when Devinely ordained law set aside the first day of the seventh month as the beginning of the religious New Year; Jewish ceremonial observances marked that day as one of prayer and devotion. Indeed, Scriptural terminology refers to it as a "Day of Memorials".[1] It is proper and fitting then, that one scan the horizon of the future on this day, as well as direct his attention to the year which has just passed into the lap of history.

As we direct our inquiring gaze into the misty realm of things-to-be, the Day of Memorials brings to mind the goals unrealized, the objectives unattained, the hopes unfulfilled, and the desires unrequited. We face the future with high resolves and resolute determination, and upon the shattered remnants of the visions of yesteryear we build new landmarks; weaving patterns for renewed endeavors.

---

1. Leviticus 23, 24.

(181)

The thoughts crowding our minds on the first day of the year help us to recall that the traditional Jewish observance of the day always inspired the pious Jew to turn his attention toward God. The first in thought, the dearest in possession, the most primary in significance, these always belonged to God in the religious evaluation of the observant Jew. This unchallenged truism appears as a softly, enchanting, musical refrain throughout the symphony of Jewish religious living.

Thus Mosaic Law consecrates the first-born unto God; the first fruit of the land is offered upon the altar of gratitude in humble recognition of God's Eternal Goodness. These gestures serve as the "recognition" of the Supremacy of the Heavenly Creator as well as the mark of nobility for men's souls that resist the temptation to arrogate unto themselves the first of the world's blessings. It was therefore in full consonance with Old Testament idealogy and in perfect accord with ancient Hebraic Lore that we joined our fellow Americans of all faiths in a special hour of prayer last Saturday.

This week we read in the Biblical selection, a remarkable incident that sheds illumination, upon the theory set forth that the first of everything should be reverently set aside for God. The story concerns itself with the migration of Jacob and with his heavy-hearted decision to forsake even temporarily the land of his fathers in order to join Joseph in Egypt. Nearing his destination, he sent Judah before him: "And he sent Judah before him unto Joseph, to direct him unto Goshen."[2] In that lean year of the seven lean years, he did not send forth his trusted son to prepare a granary. In that moment of uncertainty and trepidation he did not send a reliable agent to secure for himself the privilege of erecting a comfortable residence or for the purpose of arranging

---

2. Genesis: 46, 28.

for the means of sustenance for his large household. Nay, the purpose of Judah as interpreted by our Sages was: **L'Saken Lo Beth Talmud**......[3] "To establish a House of Learning whence knowledge and inspiration may go forth." Thus Jacob's primary concern was for the assurance of spiritual survival, a desire equally prevalent among those who first come to these shores.

The Founders of our great country caught this spirit. They recognized the primacy of things spiritual. They saw in their own position the reincarnation of the historic adventure of the Israelites as they emerged from the House of Bondage and crossed the perilous sea. In recognizing the analogy, our founders had the feeling and the conviction that the destiny of this new nation was inextricably intertwined with Biblical idealism. At this time when so many changes are wrought in the American way of life, it is well for us to remember that there was much of "Hebraic Mortar" that went into the foundation stones of America.

The Bible served as the primary source of inspiration for those who helped to bring forth the design of "A new Nation Under God", the motif of which was a nation of people, who will ever accede to and constantly acknowledge the Fatherhood of God, the Supremacy of Spirit, and the Primacy of Ideals. These, in essence, constitute the prayers which well up in our hearts at the season of the New Year. It is well to recall that in every step taken toward the establishment of the American nation, Old Testament ideals were present. When the obnoxious Stamp Act was to be denounced, hundreds of clergymen throughout the colonies preached upon the text from the Book of Esther; "And in each and every province, in every place whither the King's decree had reached, there was great mourning and wailing." When

---

3. Gen.: Rabba 95.

the fire of rebellion burst forth, they quoted the Book
of Samuel and its warring against the excesses of Kings.
Upon the Liberty Bell in Philadelphia they engraved
words from the Third Book of Moses which acted as
verbal magic and whose irridescent flow fed the flaming
jets of democratic enthusiasm.

When we consider the ideals that are among the first,
the concepts that emerge most magnificently; we must
not for a moment forget that the early settlers who
poured into this country from the four corners of the
earth came here not only because of the material advantages to be had, but also because of the opportunity
afforded for the free exercise of their religious beliefs.
It was not alone the American coin that fascinated and
attracted untold thousands, but the inscription upon the
early American coins which carried the legend: "A
Refuge to the Oppressed of All Nations."

Yea, it is for us to pray, on the turn of the calendar
year, that an end may come to calamitous days, and that
a beginning of Redemption may be at hand for all humanity. Here, too, we must direct the fondest sentiment of our hearts and the most fervent utterances of
our lips for Godliness and Divine Inspiration. May it
be our privilege to think not of glory, not of conquest, or
of aggrandizement—these are not the first fruits—but
may we direct our best efforts toward the primary ideas
of caring for the needy, feeding the hungry, healing the
wounded, and righting as far as possible the wrongs inflicted upon the helpless victims of this war. This first
above all is our fervent prayer in these times.

Amen.

ORTHODOXY'S GREATEST PROBLEM

Delivered on February 23, 1944, before a Mass Meeting of the
Orthodox Council, Syracuse, N. Y.

A T THE present time, in addition to the grave problems that confront us from without, there abide
fearful tendencies within the house of American
Israel, the challenge of which should cause justifiable
concern to those who think in terms of Jewish Spiritual
as well as Physical Survival. The growing seculariza-
tion of our Jewish institutions, and the absence of religious consideration from the councils of leading Jewish
movements, make up the severest problem gnawing at
the vitals of American Israel. This dangerous tendency
is not always apparent, nor is it readily recognizable
when it is apparent, but it is none-the-less most definitely
present, and we will do well to check its growth and
arrest its development before it expands to alarming proportions. Particularly today, when the burning needs
of our people abroad require constant and extensive
attention, must we be on guard and watch the ramparts
of our Faith against the steady encroachments of irreli-
gious forces and secular domination. We must remind
our people that when they are urged to offer a sacrifice
upon the altar of Jewish devotion, they must render
that sacrifice as a religious as well as a humanitarian
act.

Last Shabbos we read in the Torah of the establishment of Law and Justice in Israel—that is the enthronement of the Sanhedrin, in the lives of our ancestors, as
the Power Supreme, wielding temporal and Spiritual
Authority. Our Sages in the Midrash establish a close
relationship between this chapter and the final one of
the previous Biblical Portion which delineated the regu-

(185)

lations of the Mizbeach; they construed the meaning of
the laws which follow by advising that the Sanhedrin
be established in the courtyard of the Holy Temple, in
close proximity to the Mizbeach. This implies the suggested inference in the Midrashic homily wherein our
Sages impart the instruction that is most applicable to
our pressing problem—they imply, in our humble interpretation, the Lesson Supreme, that the authority of
Jewish Law the dignity of the religious Court, the power
of inspired guidance, and the influence of Spiritual
Idealism, should be found in close communion and in
harmonious relationship with the Mizbeach—the symbol
of Jewish sacrifice and self-offering.

The numerous drives, appeals, and collections, occasioned by our people's plight, stress and accentuate the
need of sacrificial giving in these critical days. They
sound the clarion call for the erection of many altars, the
building of urgently needed Mizbeachs, whereby the
means will be afforded for our devotional sharing in our
people's misery, and for our constructive effort in salvaging the broken remnants of Israel. Yet, few of
these pleas contain the basic element of Jewish religious
Law; not even one remembers the injunction: **Shetosim
sanhedrin etzel mitzbeach.**[1]

> Side by side with Jewish sacrifices, hand in hand
> with our devotional offerings, should go the Sanhed-
> rin—the authority of Jewish Law and the prestige
> of religious rule.

This appalling circumstance is the reason d'etre of
the religious wing in Zionism, which constantly declares
that sacrifices alone will build **only** a **Homeland** in Palestine—sacrifices in close harmony with the spirit of the
Sanhedrin will build a **Jewish Homeland.** We who

---

1. Exodus XXI, 2 Rashi.

dream of turning the waste and desolation of Eretz Israel into a Garden of Eden must ever be inspired by the vision of Jacob who saw a ladder firmly implanted on the ground, yet watched its highest rung reach up into the heavens.

> The land alone,—its purchase, cultivation, and improvement,—calls to mind the Mizbeach; it helps to reclaim for the Jew the **Soil** of our people; but inspiring our effort with the spirit of the Sanhedrin will return to the Jew the **Soul** of our people.

Another severely criticized aspect of American Jewish Life is the growing tendency toward the institutionalization of our charities. There is a great deal to be commended about the sincere effort of those who seek to eliminate duplicatings, correct abuses, and reduce the over-all expenditures connected with collections and drives. What will be substituted, however, for the direct contact with Jewish affairs on the part of those who a hundred times a year answer the call of a needy case, of an urgent cause, a burning issue, or a heart-rending plea? We are given a mechanical set-up which computes the cost, calculates the gains, but fails completely to take into account human and spiritual values. Greater is the tragedy and more distressing the harmful influence when we consider the scant attention paid by organized charity to Torah-true causes and institutions. They, indeed, call eloquently for sacrificial giving and ever-greater offering for the relief of misery and want. But when one considers that allocations for Yeshivos are pitifully insignificant, we must vigorously protest and organize for concerted action. American Jewish communities are systematically closed to the time-honored custom of collecting funds through responsible Meshullochim, without adequate arrangement for proper compensation to the institutions which they represent. The demands upon our consciences, for relief and rescue, are in essence a plea for the creation of a hallowed Mizbeach, yet our task will only be completed when we shall place in close congruity with it the Sanhedrin, whose presence with the Mizbeach will insure the unbroken continuity of Jewish religious existence. In its final analysis and complete evaluation, our donations become truly righteous and noble charity when they insure the observance and the honor of all our laws and sacred traditions.

Another aggravated situation, which must demand our immediate attention, is the general picture of Jewish education. In every community registration is, as a rule, frightfully small in proportion to the number of Jewish children. The problem which is within the realm of this talk, concerns itself with the tragedy of the schools that attempt to teach Hebrew as an ultimate goal, rather than as a means for the acquisition of a thorough religious training. In many of our larger cities, splendid progress is registered with the modernization of the schools; trained pedagogues and professional educators formulate high-sounding curricula, the physical aspects of the schools are greatly improved, and progressive techniques are employed. But as to the spirit of religious idealism prevalent, we must lamentably say with the Scriptures: **Rak ain yiras elokim bamokam hazeh[2]**—The Fear of God, which should be the beginning—the Foundation-stone of Jewish knowledge, is evident by its total absence.

Our children are asked to offer a sacrifice upon the altar of religious devotion, and indeed, they do when they give up two hours of every afternoon to attend Hebrew sessions while their friends play and caper in the care-free fashion of childhood. This measure of

---

2. Genesis XX, 11.

sacrifice, too, will be in vain, if the spirit of the Sanhedrin, as exemplified by religious idealism, will be removed from the Mizbeach of their offerings.

In discussing the problems of our people in the American scene, I refer to the tasks which require the proper and correct evaluation of spiritual standards in the manifestations of organized Jewish life in America. Touching upon Zionism, institutionalized charity, and Jewish education, the goal is pointed out where we must concentrate our efforts to infuse religious content and spiritual life-blood into the veins of our people. The achievement of this goal will not be simple; it will indeed take our supreme efforts and maximum strength, but it holds out a promise whose fulfilment is worthy of life's greatest adventure.

THE CHALLENGE OF JEWISH HISTORY

Broadcast over the Ministerial Association Hour, April 27, 1944

JEWISH History being in essence woven out of the texture of sacrifice, addresses its challenge to the heart of man and directs its clarion call to the nobler qualities of human nature to its higher ideals and deeper sentiments. This plea for aid to the stricken, help for the needy, relief for the sufferer, rescue for the helpless and salvation to those condemned, is based upon the unconquerable faith in the decency of our human impulses and in the trust we repose in the hearts of our people. "From every man whose heart prompted him, shall ye take My offering."[1]

This appeal is based upon the love that wells up in our hearts for those who suffer under the heel of the tyrants and when any appeal is based on Love it is addressed to the heart. Scriptures enjoin us to love the Master of the Universe—that directive too, turns first to the heart of Man as we repeat twice daily,

> "And Thou Shalt Love the Lord Thy God With All Thy Heart."[2]

This plea is not based upon the usual standards of charity, we are not asked to follow our normal philanthropic impulses; it would be unworthy of the historic tasks facing us if we would approach the problems before us with a condescending air and a patronizing sympathy. One does not pity his brother; one shares with him his last crust of bread. One does not treat his own

---

1. Exodus 25, 2.
2. Deuteronomy 6, 5.

flesh and blood with gracious condescension; one regards him with true compassion and gives him his full-hearted love. "And Man said, 'This time it is Bone of my Bones and Flesh of my Flesh' ".[3]

With the destruction of old world Jewry and the ruthless extermination of the established centers of Jewish learning, it has become the task and privilege of American Jewry to assume responsibility for those unfortunate and hounded members of our faith who have managed to escape extinction and whose very existence and relief from misery depends upon the generosity, great-heartedness and loving care that must be shown by their more fortunate brethren on this continent.

Picture the heartrending scene of a family suddenly deprived of its parents by unexpected death, and envision that tragic hour when the children are gathered around to bid their beloved a last farewell by reciting the hallowed words of the Kaddish; all eyes are turned upon the oldest son, upon whose shoulders the sorrowful legacy of assuming parental responsibility is placed. His has become the sacred task of looking after his bereaved brothers and sisters. He has become pledged to the duty of looking after them with vigilant care, tender consideration, and understanding love.

History has imposed upon us, the older brother and the older sister, the lamentful bequest of standing beside the yawning graves of our three million martyred kin whose "Blood crieth out from the earth",[4] and whose orphaned children must now become our own. It is our solemn responsibility to state before God and man, that as long as life resides within us we will serve and help those shattered remnants of our hounded and harassed

---

3. Genesis 2, 23.
4. Genesis 4, 10.

people, and for whose care and survival destiny will hold us liable.

There may be some who will quote with cold blooded cruelty and callous cynicism Cain's infamous rejoinder, "Am I MY Brother's Keeper?"[5] My conviction is firm that an overwhelming majority amongst us will cite the soothing sentiments of the Proverbs, "A brother is born for adversity",[6] and that we will rise to the heights of the privilege given us by the tides of time, and we will unflinchingly assume our designated portion of the gigantic task which we hope will enable us to see life blossom again where death and devastation now rule supreme. When we will once more see joy and happiness glow instead of the horror that has stalked in the wake of the world's most appalling terror.

Particularly now, when the forward march of the victorious Allied armies liberates more and more territory, formerly in the orbit of the common enemy, each redeemed inch of land which has become sacred with the life blood of our slaughtered ones, becomes an effective bridgehead, from which the work of relief and rescue can be accelerated. These freed areas, irrigated with their tears, offer ever increasing possibilities of redemption but they correspondingly presuppose proportionately increased responsibilities. They open before our eyes, the glorious vista of the future liberation of our enslaved people, not allowing us however to forget our mounting obligations.

But let us quote one of our national leaders.

"At times, one despairs and questions whether our people with all their good will and devotion, have

5. Ibid. 4, 9.
6. Proverbs 17, 17.

the capacity to visualize the enormity of the problems, the size of the needs, the complexity of the over-all situation, the large sums of money that are required, and the love and determination and the passionate fervor that need be brought to bear in helping our people throughout the world".

Still, in the face of these statements, I have the redoubtable faith that by harnessing the most useful talents, the most efficient energies, the most intelligent powers and the cumulative cooperative strength of our people throughout the world, and that by combining them with the ever ready helpfulness of the great humanitarian agencies, which have gained added strength with the establishment of the War Refugee Board, we can meet the challenge of the hour and snatch countless Jews from the menacing jaws of Death.

American Jewry is conducting this heroic epic in the salvaging of stricken humanity through the instrumentality of the United Jewish Appeal, an agency in whose domain are found three great national organizations. The overall agency is asking for a minimum of 32 million dollars this year to meet even part of the ever growing demand and urgency. A small share of this goal has been set aside for the National Refugee Service, an organization which has done remarkable work to help the newcomers to this land to become integrated into the social, cultural, economic life of America. In this connection, it is worthy to note that the number of refugees who have found haven and refuge upon these blessed shores is not nearly as large as the enemies of democracy would have us believe. A great many of our less fortunate brethren have demonstrated their undying gratitude to the country which has given them haven, by responding with full hearts to this nation's call, volunteering in our armed forces, while countless others con-

tributed their scientific knowledge, their technological
skill, and their industrial experience to the successful
prosecution of the war effort. Above all let us remember that with their coming to these shores they merely
retraced the steps taken by our founding fathers who in
effect and essence were the first refugees ever to arrive
in this country. It has been the heaven sent privilege
of this generation of Americans to translate into reality
the Spiritual admonition, "And Thou Shalt Love The
Stranger".

By far, a greater portion of these funds will be extended by the U.J.A., and by the United Palestine Appeal
for the upbuilding of the Jewish community in the Holy
Land. Since the advent of Hitlerism, over 300,000 of
our people, who otherwise would have fallen prey to the
Monster of Europe, have found new hope and new life
in their ancestral home land. It fills us with pride to
state that the Jewish settlements in Palestine responded
most magnificently to the war crisis, and close to thirty
thousand Jewish men and women serve with the British
forces in the Middle East, every one a volunteer. The
industrial advance occasioned by Jewish enterprises
were of unimaginable assistance to the heroic Eighth
Army as a base of supplies and in facilitating the flow of
communications. Every dollar spent in the Palestine
effort helps to transform an ancient dream into the vivid
reality of the Present and an even more glorious Future.
The character of our accomplishments in Palestine gains
enduring qualities with the realization that the funds
expended and the effort extended is not merely employed
to gain for our people surcease from misery and respite
from persecution, but that they are endowed with a sense
of achievement and with the lasting attributes that mark
ventures in nation building.

The last and the largest beneficiary of the U. J. A. is

the Joint Distribution Committee which brings aid and assistance to our co-religionists in the many lands of their exile, in the length and width of the globe, where the hope of humanity still flickers, the agents of this great organization act as the emissaries of the Jews of America, bringing healing to the sick, balm to the wounded, relief to the stricken, and a new vision to the victim buffeted about by the relentless forces of the world's greatest upheaval.

Albany's share will no doubt be raised and the goals set in this campaign should not be difficult of achievement when it is considered that every additional dollar obtained will increase the ability of American Jewry to answer the plea of those whose anguished eyes are riveted upon these shores as they murmur with their last dying breaths;

"Ours the tear filled eyes
Ours the exhausted whys
As we plead in utter desperation
How much longer yet
Shall we tears beget
Whence cometh my Salvation?"

We who will head this plea, will become the recognized agents of mercy whose prompt response will reverse the backward march of civilization and right the world's first historic wrong, by proudly stating that as long as life resides within us, we will always be, and proud to be, OUR BROTHERS' KEEPER.

With this principle guiding us, with these ideals as our source of inspiration, our lives will take on fuller meaning, as we will heed the saintly admonition of Solomon the Wise, "From all these things Guard thy heart, for out of it are the issues of life."[7]

---

7. Proverbs 4, 23.

HISTORY'S GREATEST CHALLENGE

Broadcast over the Ministerial Association Hour, April 26, 1944

IN THE history of every people, certain definite patterns are evident. To discern these patterns is the task of the historian who usually divides history into periods of static stagnation and dynamic action. As the Jew has rarely been undisturbed on his lands for a long enough period to permit the growth and decline of his creative energies, he has been of necessity in a constant state of flux, mobile and activated by his environment, spiritually alert, culturally creative, and materially energetic. The obvious pattern that served also as the leitmotif of Jewish survival was the spiritual strength and moral courage that inspired the dogged determination to hope for salvation amidst darkest despair and in the season of crushing tragedy.

Jewish history will never be understood in terms and concepts, defined by and for the convenience of historians, whether these definitions be the record of the struggle for biological survival or a series of meaningless collisions of economic, political, and racial forces. Our history represents the unfolding drama of a people's struggle for freedom against seemingly insurmountable odds. In our present international crisis, as in all troublesome periods of the past, the message of faith resurgent that stems from the challenge of history, comes not as a blind groping for something undefinable, not as a vague yearning and impotent rage, but as a genuine sorrow for the lamentful episodes of these unhappy times. This grief is fortified with a philosophical calm born of the implicit faith in Israel's destiny; in the enduring values of such permanent verities as Justice,

(196)

Righteousness, and the Dignity of Man; as exemplified by the brotherhood of all peoples, races and nations.

This challenge is addressed first to the mind of the people, who, appalled at the mounting fury of madness abroad and the rising specter of anti-Semitism a home, may lose their historical perspective and in times of national mourning and universal grief, may be shaken from their moorings and resign themselves to ultimate extinction and abject despair.   To these and others like them, the message comes from a people's saga of existence as for upward of 30 centuries, they calmed the disordered emotions of humanity distraught with the reassuring words of their religious faith:

"Even if I walk in the valley of the shadow of death, I will fear no evil."[1]

The message of our people speaks of strength in sorrow, of light through the darkness, of hope amidst despair, and it re-echoes a prophetic promise in the face of doubts and denials to a people who retain their faith notwithstanding the terrifying catastrophe that envelopes humanity today.

To you whose faith is as firm as mine
Whose trust is built in dream
I speak a word of hope divine
Omnipotent, Supreme.

These are the people whose faith remains steadfast when resignation and dismay hold sway over the human heart, who cling to the proven ideals of the past and do not surrender them to the misery of the present.   Men and women who keep faith in God and trust in their fellow-men understand the tragic experiences which impede the progress of the world and delay the fruition of our dreams and visions.   These are the ones who will

---

1. Psalm 23, 4.

murmur at a time such as now, when the danger of drifting into the shallow waters of doubt or of falling into the abyss of desperation is so close at hand:

God moves in a mysterious way
His wonders to perform
He plants His footprints upon the sea
And rides upon the storm.

History speaks in plaintive but challenging tones to those who are exposed to the influences of agnosticism and disbelief. History speaks to those who point the finger of scorn to the soul-shaking events of our age thereby indicating a planlessness for our world and a hopelessness for its inhabitants.

When friends whose image idols haunt
Sing loud to you their praise
A creepy doubt your soul doth haunt
Your eyes aloft do gaze.

The pages of our history, replete with heroic revivals from the depths of degradation, call to us in the deathless words of Moses when he addressed the embattled hosts of Israel encamped upon the banks of the Red Sea: "Fear ye not, stand still, and see the salvation of the Lord, which he will work for you today."[2] Now more than ever, do we need the reassuring belief and strengthening faith that although we fall we shall rise again; that our people suffer so that they may become the saints of God; that these are the chastisements of love, the tools used to cut the royal gem into facets of sparkling beauty, so that we may spread the word of God in its pristine purity throughout the earth. The wounds that indeed hurt deeply are the wounds of heroes whose pain is more than requited by the privilege and glory of being the spokesmen of God's law. This strong faith must

2. Exodus 14, 13.

become a personalized source of strength, the tower of our hope and the rock of our salvation:

> I, too, have friends who scorned and mocked
> The God who hides in mist
> But I stood firm though swayed and rocked
> By those who laughed and hissed.

Our thinkers speak of this faith as a spiritualized intuition, the witness of our souls, the inspiration of our people's genius. It flashes a searchlight before the unlit gate which is darkened by man's attempt to grope his way to salvation by reason and reason alone.

It devolves upon the preacher to preach, upon the teachers to teach the abiding moral lesson of our sacred religion that a slumbering faith dwells in every one of us and that we must fan that glimmering spark and make it leap forth in a blazing flame of hope. This in essence is the ultimate challenge of Jewish history echoing through the corridor of the ages, whispering into the taut ears of a pained humanity the ageless truth that our struggle for the maintenance of democracy and our sacrifices for the preservation of the rights of man shall not be in vain. We are given the right to believe that the destructive forces of satanic evil corroding the vitals of civilization will meet the historical doom which Divine Justice has assigned them.

The timeless verities of our history's challenge soothingly say that we who have survived the pre-historic paganism, the polytheism of Babylon, the esthetics of Hellinism and the sagacities of Rome, the blandishments and persecutions of the Medieval era, the religious indifference and materialism of the 19th century, will in God's good time, rise above the enemies of humanity who have reddened the skies with the blood of innocent martyrs and keep our tryst with Destiny, by helping to reintegrate the shattered cultural and spiritual forces of the world.

> With you whose faith is firm as mine
> Whose hope is built in dream
> I place my trust in God Divine
> Omnipotent, Supreme.

U. J. A. ADDRESS WORKERS' RALLY

Worcester, Mass., April 16, 1944

IT IS a special privilege to address you on the urgency of the U. J. A. because this is one of the few cities that I have visited whose leaders have taken cognizance of the ever increasing woe of our people and have set the goal for the current campaign very considerably above that of last year. Secondly, I was happy to observe that every segment of the Jewish community and every shade of opinion is working unitedly for the ultimate good that will accrue from this fund-raising campaign.

I sometimes wonder at the unwillingness or the inability of many American Jewish communities to respond adequately to the danger-signals hoisted by the enemies of our people. Numerous are the groups which continue year in and year out to make their meagre contributions without grasping the historic nature of the tasks before us. Their hearts are set stone-like and immovable, failing to respond to the needs occasioned by circumstances. Of them the prophet has spoken:

"I will remove the stony heart from within your midst. I will give thee instead a heart of flesh."[1]

The American Community should be mature enough to realize by now that we must alter our concepts of charity and philanthropy, and that our responsibilities do not end with rescuing the wanderers of the world, not even with supporting generously our blossoming Jewish community in the Holy Land. Our obligations must, of necessity, include the unstinting support of Jewish reli-

---

1. Ezekiel XXXVI, 26.

gious institutions here in our own blessed United States, the establishment and cultivation of Jewish educational centers, and the proffering of extended sustaining strength to all groups and organizations that foster an unflinching interest in the present and future of American Israel. All of this, and more, is part and parcel of your Federation Campaign.

Another pleasant feature of this gathering is the assurance given me by your distinguished leaders, that instead of the usual fragmentation which is the bane of so many American Jewish communities, this inspired group of workers is actually a cross section of Worcester Jewry. It should be so, since the work of rescue and relief does not recognize differences of opinion, distinction of classes, or differentiation amongst the various strata of our religious Jewish groupings.

Once before a princely son of our people construed his migration to the land of Egypt as a Heaven-planned mission for the rescue of his brethren in the famine years which were to follow:

This generation of American Israel has been bequeathed the sad though exalted task of plucking the remnant of European Jewry from the crucible of fire into which the events of the last few years have cast them. As the Josephs of our generation, it behooves us to consider for a moment some salient features of the life of that dreamer, whose dramatic rise from the depths of the dread dungeons to the heights of royal adventure constitutes one of the most remarkable incidents in the life-story of our people. We remember the Biblical story telling of the favor and preference shown unto Joseph by his grieving father, Jacob, who expressed his choice by making for his beloved son a coat of many colors. What an object of envy this little shirt became.

As the tragic denouement unfolds before our eyes, we hear that the vengeful brothers remark anent the arrival of the unsuspecting Joseph:

"Do you recognize it, father? Is this the garment of your son? We found it in the fields."[2]

Jacob took the torn and blood-stained garment tenderly into his arms, and with his eyes flooded with tears and his voice broken with the surging sobs welling up from within him, he said:

"Joseph, my beloved Joseph, devoured by wild beasts."[3]

History has called us to task and has exacted bloody payment for that act of disunity and disloyalty amongst the tribes of Israel. That shirt, woven from skeins of fatherly love, it's colors hued by tears shed because of the untimely death of Rachel, has turned into a thing of knotted cords of venom, thus replacing the material of the texture of love with the fabric of sheer hate. Every color of that fateful shirt has been heard from at the bitter roll-call of the persecutors of our people. The Brown shirts of Nazidom, the faded Black shirts of Italy, and the Gold shirts of Mexico,—they have all exacted their toll from our brethren in payment of an old sin. Your united effort and the united expression of our people all over the world is the only solution to the problems engendered by the hatreds of our times.

Our response to the appeal of Jewish misery will help wipe out the bloody stains on the tattered garment of Israel, and will weave once more into a unified texture the scattered portions of Israel's cloth.

---

2. Genesis **XXXVII, 33.**
3. Ibid. 34.

You who are entrusted with the obligation of knocking at the doors of the Jewish Community, do not face an easy task. Tell the people, when you see them, that their help and assistance will make the sun shine once again where darkness reigns. Great as your task is, still greater is the compensation of knowing that for every step that you take, some Jewish person somewhere will walk again. I bespeak to you the blessings of God. May His Gracious Presence accompany you on your hallowed mission. Go forth, enthused by the power and idealism of this sacred cause and invigorated by the strength of your convictions.

May the Lord prosper your efforts, and may'st Thou, O Heavenly Father, Bless these messengers of mercy with the Sustaining Strength of Thy Holiness. Spread before them the Light of Thy Countenance, and may they and the people in whose behalf they go forth, cross safely the sea of tribulation as our forefathers crossed the tempestuous sea through Thy Gracious Will. Prosper the endeavors of these, Thy humble servants, who are indeed

> Thy Poets O Lord
> A Pilgrim Band
> Lighting high hopes
> Above a darkened land.

ADDRESS DELIVERED AT THE DINNER OF THE JEWISH COMMUNITY OF LOWELL, MASS.

On May 2, 1944, on behalf of the United Jewish Appeal

THE response of American Jewry to the historic tasks occasioned by the tides of the times has been both severely censured and fully lauded. There are those who consider our answer to the challenge, flung at us by the world-wide tentacles of Hitlerism, as pale, puny, and powerless, while there are others who point to the splendid achievement of the National Refugee Services. They recount with pride the saving efforts of the Joint Distribution Committee, and glory in the magnificent endeavors of our pioneers in the Holy Land. The truth, perhaps, lies between these two extreme attitudes, and a fair evaluation of our work for rescue will probably reveal that although we did not ignore the plea addressed to us, we have not comprehended in full measure the impact of the times.

Our greatest failure, however, lies in not grasping the possibilities dormant in the effort of our many agencies to save at least the innocent young ones whose escape from the jaws of death could be made more readily possible by a greater intensification of effort and deeper comprehension of the tasks confronting us. We, too, like the brothers of Joseph who thought him dead must say, as we examine our consciences: **Avol ashemim anachnu**—"But we are sinful",[1] and we were negligent with regard to the little ones whose special guardian angels we should be privileged to consider ourselves. There are untold incidents that can be cited in relation to the above, but to my mind comes a story told recently

---

1. Genesis XLII, 21.

in the "Jewish Spectator." According to that version, in some part of Southeastern Europe, two trains stopped simultaneously on adjoining tracks, though headed in opposite directions. One carried a load of our unfortunate people bound to the Polish Ghettoes and certain extinction, while the other was crammed full of passengers who were being saved and bound for Eretz Israel. As the passengers of these two railway trains talked to one another, one mother, bound for the slaughter houses of Poland, handed a little infant huddled in her arms to a fellow Jewess whose destination was Palestine. I leave it to you, dear friends, to see with your own spiritual eyes, the feelings, sentiments, and emotions experienced by these two Jewish women. If we were able to bring into this room the last dying gasps of countless martyred brethren and sisters, the words most audible, unquestionably would be their desperate plea to save those of their innocent offspring who are still in the realm of the living.

Let us for a moment conjure up the vision of our own homes, where a dearly beloved child of ours may be ill and suffering pain. Look into his troubled eyes and multiply the pained expression upon his countenance a million fold, and you will get an idea of the piercing cry and the shrieking terror that knock at our hearts for merciful deliverance and compassionate rescue. The story is told about the late Rabbi, Simon Soffer, former Chief Rabbi of Krakow, who once led a delegation of Galician Jewish deputies to the Emperor Franz Josef imploring that ruler to order the cessation of the injustices perpetrated upon the Jews of that province. When the sainted scholar was reminded by a court attache that his voice was too loud in the presence of the Emperor, Rabbi Soffer thus addressed himself to the ruler of Austria Hungary: "Your Majesty is familiar, probably, with the story in the Old Testament about the birth and discovery of Moses. The Scripture relates that when the fair princess of Egypt opened the basket that contained the babe, she cried: 'Behold a child is crying',[2] and immediately thereafter the daughter of Pharoah remarked:

And she said: "He is of the Hebrew Children".[3]

Strangely enough, the Biblical terminology first speaks of a child, and her comment is expressed in the plural: **Miyaldai** thereby imparting the lesson that though technically only Moses was crying, his bitter anguish and despairing whimpers reflected the woeful cry of thousands doomed to slavery. "My voice may have sounded loud, but it was not because it was disrespectful, nor was it due to a lack of appreciation of the proprieties that one must observe in the presence of his sovereign, but in the plea which I bring to his Majesty today are the echoes from the muffled cries and subdued tears of two million Jews who suffer political disabilities, religious restrictions, and economic hardships." Yea, multiply the cry of one child by several million, and you will get a faint notion of the heart-piercing woe that comes to us from the sorrowing hearts of those who are about to die.

I have seen refugee children come off the boat in Miami, Florida. They had lived with misery by day, and had slept with terror at night. Even after they had become accustomed to some of the most elementary manifestations of Americanism, the least little reminder of their former sufferings brought evident horror into their emaciated faces. Whether it was a policeman's uniform, or their first bus ride, or a visit to the park, or anything that recalled to them their former humiliation

2. Exodus II, 6.
3. Ibid.

and degradation, it filled their little faces with the anguish of the ages. Well has Raskin described the child of the ghetto:

> He plays, he capers like a child
> But oft it seems to you
> That in a moment he will grow
> An old and wandering Jew.

It takes, approximately, one thousand dollars of American currency, a great deal of wire-pulling extensive and intensive by the JBC representatives in Europe, and the love and welcoming arms of the Jews in Palestine, to save a single child from the nightmare which is Europe. But still, when I come to the different communities in which the United Jewish Appeal campaigns are conducted, I find it difficult to convince the local leaders that every thousand dollars added to their goal may mean the saving of an additional Jewish life. In the words of our Sages: **Kol hamkayem Nefesh achas meyisroel** with the rescue of every additional Jewish youngster, we can help build a new world for them, a far better future and a far happier lot than would otherwise have been their fate.

HANDS ACROSS THE SEA

U. J. A. Address delivered at Patterson, N. J., May 15, 1944.

THE number of appeals that are addressed to our people in these times of storm and stress have caused many to think of their obligation toward their faith in terms of charity, and charity only. An old fallacy is thus disinterred, and we hear time and again the point of view which maintains that one's contributions to Jewish charitable causes serves as a barometer in determining the degree of his Jewishness. While this attitude is manifestly mistaken, its corollary is unquestionably true. No one can possibly be called a good Jew unless he or she actively participates in the relief and rescue work which is one of the major notes in the song of Jewish survival.

As a stranger who is privileged to speak in your midst for a holy cause, I am compelled to accept this as the sole frame of reference as to the degree of your Jewishness. The standard of judgment which will guide my opinion will be influenced solely by your response to the bloody cry of our innocent martyrs whose plea for salvation can be ignored only by those who are willing and prepared to renounce their affiliation with the community of Israel. The story is told of a young man who was suspected of suffering from a heart ailment, and when he visited a noted specialist in that field, the doctor asked for his hand. The patient was puzzled by the query and wanted to know why the eminent physician did not examine his heart first. "Show me your hand," he was told, "and I will know a great deal about the condition of your heart."

(209)

I may not be a very great specialist in my chosen pro-
fession, but I can tell the warmth, the humanity, and
the Jewishness of your hearts, by looking at your hands
and discerning therein the measure of our devotion and
the maturity of your judgment. This manner of determining Jewish loyalties has been effectively employed
ever since crises and emergencies have taxed our people's
ability to survive the onslaught of our enemies.

When Jeremiah sat on the ruins of Jerusalem and
poured the anguish of his soul into the bitter lament of
the Book of Tears, he grieved over the abject misery of
the present, and, simultaneously he sought to express
some measure of hope and to find some source of solace
and comfort. And thus spake Jeremiah:"Let us lift up
our hearts with our hands unto God in the heavens".[1]

The prophet speaks to us today also, and reminds us
that we can come before God only if the offerings of our
hearts have materialized in the contributions of our
hands—the Rabbis of the Talmud have gone a step
further, and, from the verse quoted above, have deducted
the abiding lesson that "No prayer is answered for any
person unless his heart is in his hands";[2] indeed, King
David gave the quotation still further meaning in the
statement that our lives, our souls, and our salvation
must ever be in the palms of our hands. **Nafshi b'chapai
thomid.**[3]

I don't think it necessary to tell this group in grue-
some detail about the suffering, the horror, the mortal
anguish experienced by those of our brethren who survived the fiendish persecutions and brutal extermina-
tion-attempts which have become the lot of the Jews of

---

1. Lamentations III, 41.
2. Talmud, Tannith VIIIa.
3. Psalms CXIX, 109.

Europe. Recently I read a tragic tale of a refugee child in Palestine who drowned while swimming in a creek. The Chalutzim of the community and the Jews from neighboring colonies sobbed and wept copiously over the little body of one who had had the good fortune to escape the hell of Europe—only to die in such a manner. The Friends of the little victim stood around silently, and when one of them was asked why he didn't cry he replied, "I am used to the dead, I used to sleep among them."

American Jewry is charged with the task of bringing back to life those who still sleep with the dead, and those who are consigned to join them unless immediate and energetic steps are taken. Those thousands of children for whom immigration visas can be obtained must be rescued. Passports will be secured for them by the officially accredited agency known as the War Refugee Board, a group which has done a magnificent piece of work in its quiet way. To help this group, the importance of having the heart in the hand cannot be overestimated. The enormous significance of the show of your hands can be illustrated by the story of a hermit dwelling on a mountain top. He was famed for his wisdom and honored for his kindness and humanity. A young man living in a neighboring village decided to test this paragon of virtue and wisdom. He approached the old man with his two hands enclosing an object. He was determined to have the hermit decide what it was he held within his hands. He asked "What have I here between my hands?" The old man replied, "From the manner in which your hands are placed, you are holding a bird or some other such creature." The object in his hand was indeed a tiny helpless trembling bird. It was still alive, but the fellow was determined to prove the old man wrong by crushing its little life out of it if the hermit should guess that it was alive, and by letting

15

it live if he should say it was dead. So, with much confidence, the scoffer asked, "Is it alive or dead?" The old hermit slowly replied, "As you will it my son, as you will it, for it is in your hands, and the decision rests with you."

My fellow Jews, it is no exaggeration to state and no mere rhetoric to proclaim, that it is within the power of your hands to decide the fate and destiny of our helpless brothers and sisters overseas. If you hold your hands tightly closed, they will perish; if you open them wide, they will live again, and praise the name of the God above whose messengers of mercy you are privileged to be. Open your hands, and let them show the measure of the warmth in your hearts!

THE FIRST BLESSING OF OUR DAYS

Address delivered at the Jewish Education Day Rally
Newburgh, New York, September 24, 1944

THERE is much to recommend in your program for
propagandizing the start of the new Season in your
Hebrew School at the time when our religious New
Year is ushered in. It reminds the members of your
community of the great advantage to be gained by starting early, and it impresses upon the minds of your people the need for an increased emphasis on educational
values, where it does most good.

It is generally conceded that we have been amiss in
the last few generations in estimating properly the value
of a thoroughly integrated system of religious education.
Looking at the problem from the broad historical perspective, I am reminded of a most profound observation by
the revered teacher, the late Dr. Bernard Revel of
Blessed Memory. He interpreted the causes of our
greatly weakened position by tracing the historical
sequence of the growth of Jewish settlement in this
blessed land. Basing his summation upon the injunction of the Mishna that our wall stands and survives on
three mighty pillars: **Torah, abodah, gemiluth chasodim,** [1]
our revered master explained that the first wave of
Jewish immigration to this country, in the wake of the
Spanish conquerers, and the newcomers that came from
Spanish lands, built the first Synagogues in the Western
Hemisphere. All of us recount with reverence the historic import attached to the Shearith Israel in New York,
the old Synagogue in Newport, and the manifold bene-
factions of Judah Touro, but these hardly pioneers con-

---

1. Aboth I, 2.

centrated on only one phase of the Mishnaic injunctions and in stressing Abodah they did not leave us a legacy including the other two pillars.

The next large migration of our co-religionists came from western Europe, particularly from Germany. Arriving about the middle of the last century, these newcomers who brought with them industriousness and a liberal spirit emphasizing the socialogical aspect of our great traditions, stressed in their communal endeavors, charitable institutions and public welfare agencies. This accentuated emphasis on **Gemiluth chasodim** left a noble legacy and the care for the immediate indigent was provided for by their far-sighted leadership.

It was not until the wide masses of eastern European Jewry, coming in the closing decades of the 19th century, arrived in large numbers, that the Torah was assigned its position of primacy. Our leading Hebrew Educational Institutions, and all our Yeshivos grew out of the efforts of this teaming mass of belated arrivals who brought with themselves an irresistible desire to transplant the study of the Torah to these hospitable shores. The sombre fact that only a pathetically small faction of American Jewish Life is effected by the Torah Spirit can no doubt be traced to the lamentable fact that the founding of Torah institutions, which in the order of their eminence came **first** in Rabbi Simon's Dictum, was only **last** attended to when that broad segment of Jewish life was established in the Western World. The sad realization that vast areas of Jewish existence are entirely unoccupied by the influence of religious practices has its foundation in the belated start of our educational endeavors.

Discouraging as this historical development has been by itself, we have suffered still additional spiritual losses which grew directly out of the tempo of American life. The exaggerated emphasis placed upon material advancement has led to a woeful negligence even among groups where the desire was latent for cultural gain. To borrow an idiom currently used, American Jewry has done too little and even that came too late. The appalling ignorance of our youth with its resultant calamities made itself apparent in the wide steam of Jewish Life, and the belatedly aroused conscience of our people hastily raised the barricades that aimed to check the stampede and halt the exodus by the establishment of social and recreational agencies under Jewish auspices. The rapid growth of Youth Peoples associations and Community Centers is the palliative with which our frightened leaders attempt to compensate for their failure to implant in the hearts of our young people a love for things religious. Without impinging in the least upon the usefulness of these institutions, it will be readily granted that their scope is confined, their reach circumscribed, and their influence fragmentary. No amount of professional "Youth Building", "Technical Orientation", and "Social Adjustment", courses can substitute for cultural illiteracy and for the lack of religious cohesiveness. To attain the latter we must begin early enough with instruction in the home, continue effectively with education in religious schools, and integrate it successfully in the organized activities of maturing years.

The Rabbis of the Talmud in an interesting discussion call our attention to the Primacy of Torah in our peoples existence. They refer to the loss of our independent nationhood and furtively inquire **Mipneh mah ovdoh haaretz**[2]—"Why was our land lost to us?" The unequivocal answer is **Mipneh shelo borchu batorah techiloh**[3]—

---

2. Talmud Baba Meziah 85a.
3. Ibid.

"Because the men of that generation failed to recite the blessing of the Torah early upon arising."

When we review the loss of whole generations from active Jewish life, when we seek to ascertain the responsibility for the appalling lack of Jewish consciousness, When we must perforce admit that a vast majority of our young people think of their religion only in terms of some faint, vestigial, residue of religious observances, harking back to Bar Mitzvah preparations, then we too must confess our guilt and shamefully proclaim that **Shelo borchu batorah techiloh.**

In their formative years, our children are neglected, the first years of their conscious existence, the early expression of their ability, the first ideals which they are taught to cherish, the primary training which they receive, the first blessing indeed of their lives, is not for Torah. Hence the great loss we suffered, and hence the immense ground which must be recovered.

I am therefore doubly gratified to witness the wholehearted effort expended by your illustrious rabbi, the leaders of your community, and the teachers of your religious school, who arranged this imposing rally to mark the beginning of a new school year. With these acts, you rightfully place the emphasis on the early and impressionable years where it justly belongs, thus commencing the mighty battle to regain the lost areas of Jewish interest and raise with the help of the Living God a **Dor yeshorim y'vorach**[4]—"A generation of the Blessed and of the Righteous." Amen.

---

4. Psalms 112, 2.

HE MADE THE WHITEHOUSE A LIGHTHOUSE FOR HUMAN HOPES

**Memorial Address Preached April 15, 1945 at
Congregation Beth El Jacob, Albany, N. Y.**

"IT IS good to give thanks unto the Lord."[1] With this quotation from the Book of Psalms did our late lamented president introduce his first war-time Thanksgiving Message in the very uncertain days of November, 1942. Surely we could do no less in this solemn moment when we gather to honor the memory of Franklin Delano Roosevelt, than to register our grateful appreciation that by the grace of God, he was at the helm of our country during the twelve most momentous years of its history. The personal grief that we nevertheless feel is too deeply etched in everyone's soul to require elaboration, and we must be careful lest in the moment of overpowering sorrow we forget to offer our bountiful thanks for having been permitted to bask in the vivid glow of his personality and to live securely in a Democratic society which prospered under his fearless leadership.

Though it may sound presumptuous on my part, none the less I am convinced that if the man of the kind heart, of the infectious smile, of the warm generous disposition, could speak to us now, he would no doubt assure us that he wants us to honor the day of his departure from our midst with Tennyson's immortal lines:

> Sunset and evening Star
> And one clear call for me
> And may there be no mourning at the bar
> When I put out to sea.

---

1. Psalms 92, 2.

II

The historian of the future who will write with cool detachment and calm deliberation will be best equipped to sum up his enduring achievements and lasting accomplishments. Even we can readily enumerate, however, that he brought us through the most critical depression in our history, led us successfully toward victory in history's most devastating war, and he brilliantly demonstrated that the free will of a Democratic people can cope with the sharpest crisis in a world ridden with baneful dictatorships.

To those who mourn that he did not see us through to complete victory, I quote King Solomon's picturesque assurance: **K'shoshano ben hachochim**[2]—"He was like a rose between the thorns." Well we may quote the philosophy of Alphonso Carr: "Some people always find fault with God for putting thorns on roses; I always thank Him for putting roses on thorns."

That both President Roosevelt and those who believed in him had a thorny road to traverse, nowise lessens the exalted fragrance of his magnificent qualities which were symbolized by the majestic rose. One of his greatest tributes will be the realization that though the vituperative cannibalism of politics snapped at him at times with insane fury, and though the mounting disasters of humanity shook the very foundations of the earth, he remained serene while others grew tumultuous, clear of vision while others were confused, undeviating while others were erratic. He was secure in his democratic faith, while others doubted, certain in his orbit while others floundered hopelessly in the treacherous mire of politics and diplomacy.

---

2. Song of Songs 2, 2.

III

In the Biblical selections read in our Synagogues yesterday, we were acquainted with the functions and purposes of the Kohen, the Priest in ancient Jewish Rituals, who had a special responsibility when the dreaded plague of leprosy made its appearance.[3]

These plagues were generally classified in three categories: those of Nigei Odom—Assailing people, Nigei Bais —Those attacking human residence, and Nigei Beged— Those encroaching upon the clothing and habiliments of people. Many of our commentators interpret these to be manifestations of moral leprosy where the physical rehabilitation that followed in the wake of the Priest's ministrations, was coupled with spiritual regeneracy. That these plagues were conspicuous in our days need not be argued, but that Franklin Delano Roosevelt saw them in their full horror will forever remain his greatest tribute. We remember that significant expression in his classic Second Inaugural when he spoke with concern over the fact that "One third of the nation was ill-housed, ill-clad, ill-nourished", thus attacking boldly all three classes of **Negoim** which were gnawing away at the very vitals of our people's existence.

Our rabbis significantly comment that a great benefit redounded to our ancestors who set themselves earnestly to the task of destroying the homes thus plagued: for in so doing they discovered untold wealth hidden by the former owners of Canaan.[3a] Similarly can we gratefully recount that because our great erstwhile president had resolutely set himself the obligations to eradicate these modern plagues, he left unto us an untold legacy of physical wealth and spiritual gains.

---

3. Leviticus, Chapters 12 and 13.
3a. Talmud Horioth 10.

He gave new hope to a desperate people and at the same time enriched the nation with a magnificent network of roads, a wonderful development of parks, a splendid expansion of schools, urgently needed hospitals which carried over and became the blessed results of a wretched depression. He, like our Master Moses many centuries before, found the people murmuring because of the bitter waters and, like the Hebrew Law-Giver, he cast the trees over the expanse which sweetened the bitter waters.[4]

The future will adequately recount that the marvelous program of reforestation, soil control, and civilian conservation, not only changed the physical landscape of America, not alone did it give several million young people a new hope, but it considerably sweetened the bitter waters of adversity which plagued our people in the early thirties. This courageous leader, who had the makings of greatness in his fibre, rose to the full stature of his greatness when the times demanded it, and electrified a moribund people with winged words of soaring hope. In this hour of America's great grief, we, his countrymen whose proud champion he was, take heart from the inspired realization that the courageous leadership of our great president not only made him the symbol of humanity here at home but that with his all-embracing love for his fellowmen he succeeded in making the Whitehouse a Lighthouse for human hopes **everywhere.**

IV

There is a final thought which is especially timely today and compels articulation. Eighty years ago on this day of April 15th, Abraham Lincoln breathed his last after a night of agony and a life of suffering. There is

---

4. Exodus 15, 25.

much in common between the trials and tribulations of these two martyred presidents. To quote from the Gettysburg Address is therefore most timely. The words, "That these honored dead shall not have died in vain", certainly take on meaning when we must dedicate ourselves to the sacred obligations for putting into reality the blue-prints for peace worked out by our late president. Then too, "From these honored dead, we take increased devotion". The honor to Franklin D. Roosevelt's memory will best be expressed if we accept his martyred life as a new source of devotion from whence we draw the inspiration to give meaning to his faith in Democratic processes.

It was symbolic of his great love of the outdoors, of his dogged attachment to the land he loved, that the end came to him under God's blue heaven, while he was looking at far horizons, basking in the glow of his coming sunset. Behind him stood the clear silhouettes of the paths he trod—before him stretched the unknown mysteries of Life eternal, as if in his last conscious mortal moments, he wanted to cast one more lingering look upon the country for whose welfare he sacrificed so much and for whose benefit he too offered his best years, to make sure the promise of former days which effectively holds that, "Government of the people, for the people, and by the people, shall not perish from the earth", would remain true.

IN MEMORIAM
RABBI JACOB A. HORWITZ

TAMMUZ 5, 5703
Preached at Congregation Beth El Jacob

M Y SORROWFUL friends, it is difficult to measure words correctly when one eulogizes a departed leader in Israel. Speaking here where the sincere words of Rabbi Horwitz rang out during the many years of his distinguished ministry, I quote the Talmudic testimonial: **Kothlei beth hamidrosh yochichu** —Let the walls of this edifice testify, let them offer the eloquent testimony of flowery garlands in tribute to the years of service that he gave to this congregation and to the community. Now, especially, when Jewry the world over is subjected to torment and torture, we can ill afford the loss of such men as our revered and departed Rav.

II

It is a thankless and unrewarded task to be a Spiritual leader in a world where materialistic considerations rank supreme. It was many times more so several decades back when the living waters of the Torah had to be drawn from barren rocks and solid stone. In the midst of an unsettled society which was a seething caldron of heterogeneous elements, ruled over by a babel of voices, precious few could claim that they would not say, as our Master Moses said, and we read it in this week's Biblical Portion: **Shimu-no hamorim Haminhasela haze notzi lochem moyim**—"Hear ye now, rebels, are we to bring you forth water out of this rock?"[2] Yet,

---

2. Numbers, XX, 17.

even under such circumstances, our revered Rabbi tried
to maintain a friendly smile and benevolent attitude
which endeared him to every strata in the community,
every shade of opinion, every level of intelligence. We
may say of him as it was said of the first High Priest in
Israel, whose demise is recorded in the current Portion
of the Law, that

"They wept for Aaron for thirty days, even the
whole House of Israel."[3]

Our Sages in the Midrash sensed an added implication in
the seemingly superfluous word **Kol** meaning all, for
usually the people were referred to as **Beth Israel,** The
House of Israel. The implication they deduce from this
added word is that not only the men, but women and
children as well, mourned him, since they all loved his
peaceful ways, admired his blessed temperament, and
revered his noble demeanor.[4] Let our finest expression
of tribute rest on similarly high grounds of idealism,
and may the stricken family be consoled in the knowledge that although the Crown of Glory is removed from
their midst, the honor extended to their father is in the
light of the one accorded to the first Cohen Godol in
Israel.

III

In the moving eulogies spoken by my honored colleagues from the Capitol District, we heard from men
in the Rabbinate who were associated with the late Rabbi
Horwitz for many many years. They spoke of two
striking attributes in his character and accentuated the
beneficial consequences that resulted from the constant
application of these characteristics. They told us that

3. Numbers, XX, 29.
4. Ibid. Midrash Rabba.

though he, like Aaron Hacohen, was fond of peace, he
would not sacrifice one iota of his convictions, neither
would he suppress the Truth nor truckle with privilege
for the attainment of peace. The prophetic ideal
attributed to the High Priest was ever his guiding light.

"The Law of Truth was in his mouth, and unright-
eousness was not found on his lips."[5]

Parallel with his desire to follow in the path of uncom-
promising Truth, there was in his nature gracious kindli-
ness which was especially overflowing toward the
younger colleagues who came under the orbit of his influence. However, he did not spare this **Chesed** from
anyone who sought his helping hand, and numerous are
the instances when he sought out the situation to offer a
helping hand before he was even approached. Truly
these twin attributes of **Chesed** and **Emeth** were encased in the name which was his in this world. The prophet characterizes our Grandfather Abraham with the
admirable trait of Kindness, for he opened his doors
wide for every passing stranger; and he ascribes stern
Truthfulness to Jacob who even on his death-bed casti-
gates the wrong-doer and rebukes the evil-minded.
Titen Emeth l'yaakov chesed l'avrohom[6]—Avrohom
Yaakov Horwitz possessed a handsome quantity of both
of these Divine Virtues, for in his soul Kindness and
Truth met together as is the dream of the Psalmist.
Chesed—voemeth nifgoshu.[7]

We, who enjoyed his friendship, learned from his experience, and basked in the reflected glory of his splendid personality, stand with bowed heads and bereaved
souls before his bier, and our greatest consolation is in
the holy conviction that in the Heavens Above, where

5. Malachi II, 6.
6. Mica VII, 20.
7. Psalms LXXXV, 11.

Justice is triumphant and Virtue reigns supreme, there awaits him the Eternal Reward of the Crown of Glory forged through the painful process of an earthly pilgrimage. May the **Chesed** in his heart and the **Emeth** in his soul await him in the Academy on High with the companionship of the souls of the Saints and Righteous men of all ages. **Chesed v'emeth y'kadmu fonecho.**[8]

May the Holy One of Israel Who is a Father of Orphans and a Comforter of widows console the bereaved family amidst the mourners of Zion and Jerusalem.

---

8. Psalms LXXXIX, 15.

CPSIA information can be obtained
at www.ICGtesting.com
Printed in the USA
BVHW091914050220
571510BV00005B/285